For the first time ever, 20 of the greatest legends in ᴜ⌣⌣ history are exclusively profiled in this star-studded companion to the RTÉ radio series, Gaelic Football's Top 20.

Among the interviewees are Kerry legend Mick O'Connell and Galway's Seán Purcell, who vividly recount Gaelic football's golden age in the 1950s and '60s, while Seán O'Neill describes Down's historic breakthrough in 1960.

The great Kerry teams of the '70s and '80s are also represented by stars including Pat Spillane, Mikey Sheehy, Jack O'Shea, John Egan and Eoin Liston, while Dublin's Jimmy Keaveney and Brian Mullins assess their most memorable battles with the Kerry giants.

Elsewhere in the book, Larry Tompkins and Billy Morgan revisit Cork's matches with Meath in the late '80s and early '90s, Meath's Colm O'Rourke and Martin O'Connell offer their view of the contests and Offaly are represented by Matt Connor. Donegal's Martin McHugh and Derry's Anthony Tohill recall their breakthroughs, unlike Mayo's Willie Joe Padden and Sligo's Mickey Kearins, who instead describe the pain of their counties' near misses. On a different note, Enda Colleran remembers Galway's famous three-in-a-row in the '60s.

Gaelic Football's Top 20 is crammed with anecdotes of the great contests and controversies that have dominated Gaelic football in the last half a century. Offering rare insights and behind-the-scenes analysis, it is essential reading for all fans of Ireland's most popular sport.

For Seán

MAINSTREAM SPORT

GAELIC FOOTBALL'S TOP 20

COLM KEANE

MAINSTREAM
PUBLISHING
EDINBURGH AND LONDON

This edition, 2004

First published in Great Britain in 2003 by
MAINSTREAM PUBLISHING COMPANY (EDINBURGH) LTD
7 Albany Street
Edinburgh EH1 3UG

ISBN 1 84018 886 3

A catalogue record for this book is available from the British Library

Typeset in Berkeley and Gill Sans Condensed

Printed in Great Britain by
Cox & Wyman Ltd

CONTENTS

INTRODUCTION

EARLY IMAGES OF MICK O'CONNELL SHOW HIM SOARING TO THE SKY, HIS ARMS outstretched, reaching out to the heavens in search of the elusive leather ball. Those photographs, invariably in black and white, define the purity and quality of an era. Those were the days when backs stayed back and forwards focused on their dedicated tasks. It also was a time when individual skills superseded team dynamics, when high fielding and long kicking outshone team effort, when great moments of personal triumph marked the high points of a game.

Those images of Mick O'Connell epitomise an era that was coming to a close almost four decades ago. It was, in many ways, the end of Gaelic football's age of innocence. In its place came a new brand of football based on speed, fast passing, quickly taken frees and interlocking movements. New stars emerged who were masters of the running game. Dedicated sharpshooters and extraordinarily powerful midfield giants arrived on the scene. Although linked to the past by great players like Mick O'Connell, Seán Purcell and Seán O'Neill, the new practitioners played a brand of Gaelic football light years distant from that which went before.

Back in the 1950s and early 1960s, who could have predicted the massive transformation that was about to occur in Gaelic football? Who could have foreseen the emphasis on speed, fitness and athleticism that would dominate the game? Who could have spotted the team dynamics, squad rotation, strength-in-depth that would characterise the modern era? Just as importantly, who could have identified the huge impact of commerce, sponsorship and advertising, the sale of television rights and the huge support mechanisms of physiotherapists, psychologists, team doctors and managers that would become central to the game of Gaelic football?

Throughout these evolutions, revolutions and transformations one factor remained unchanged throughout the ages. It matters not whether the era in question gave prominence to great fielders, devastating sharpshooters, overlapping wing-backs or canny corner-forwards. Nor does it matter whether the style of football seemed closer to basketball or rugby than to the high fielding of an earlier age. Whatever the era or style, the fact is that Gaelic football unfailingly produced great stars; titanic footballers who dominated games and whose talent and finesse stood out throughout the decades. These were players who adorned young fans' bedroom walls; whose moves were copied by small boys on the playing fields of Ireland. Novice players were transformed into budding Jimmy Keaveneys, Pat Spillanes or Mikey Sheehys. Football in every county drew a seemingly inexhaustible supply of stars from among its amateur ranks that kept the spirit of the game alive.

Nobody can doubt the contribution made by great players to Gaelic football. The passion and self-sacrifice, the battle to overcome pain and recover from near-fatal injury are a common thread in these players' lives. The thrill of walking out into Croke Park, the homecomings and celebrations, the heartbreaks and disappointments at realising that the game's honours would elusively pass them by are an ever-present. The ambitions of players like Jack O'Shea and Brian Mullins who, as youngsters, dreamed of being like Mick O'Connell are a mainstay of the game. Aspirations of scoring in All-Ireland finals, of honouring parents' expectations, of bringing pride to clubs, villages and counties are the backbone of what we have come to know and love about Gaelic football.

Without any doubt, the 20 players whose stories are contained between these covers are some of the finest who have ever played the game. Their stories track the evolution of a sport that, influenced by the arrival of Australian football and the pressures of television, changed from the slow, ponderous game of the first half of the twentieth century to the speed of the century's last three decades. Exploiting the hand-pass and inspired by legendary figures like Eoin Liston and John Egan, the great Kerry team of the late 1970s produced a brand of football that many perceived to be closer to basketball than to the traditional Gaelic game. Nobody can doubt that team's greatness. Nor can anyone question the quality of teams like Seán O'Neill's Down in 1960 and Enda Colleran's Galway a little later on, not to mention the wonderfully talented Dublin side that was Kerry's near-nemesis in the 1970s.

There were other great teams: Meath and Cork in the late 1980s and early 1990s, Offaly in 1982, Donegal in 1992 and Derry in 1993. Those teams possessed great players like Matt Connor, Colm O'Rourke, Martin O'Connell, Larry Tompkins, Martin McHugh and Anthony Tohill. Former All-Ireland winner Billy Morgan coached one of them to a historic double. Some of those sides made temporary breakthroughs, basking for a moment in the sunshine of championship success. Others put together short runs, briefly emulating those great counties like Kerry and Dublin that had traditionally dominated the championship. All were great sides, each deserved their moment of glory and all produced wonderful players who lit up the firmament with their dazzling skills. We owe them all a debt of gratitude.

There are many people to be thanked for their help in compiling this book. In particular, the players who are profiled, together with their wives and families, afforded me the sort of welcome and hospitality long associated with Gaelic games. Like hurling, Gaelic football is full of kind and dedicated people who are committed to the sport and who are willing to give of their time. I received enormous help from various GAA county officials, among them Patrick Teehan from Offaly, Noreen Doherty from Donegal, Donal McCormack from Down, Miko Kelly from Galway, Jim Forbes from Cork, Patsy Mulholland from Derry, Tommy Kilcoyne from Sligo and Seán Feeney from Mayo. GAA Headquarters in Dublin were generous with their contacts, as were many GAA county offices around the country, especially in Meath and Donegal.

Many hundreds of people, ranging from former and current players and administrators to commentators and ordinary fans, willingly gave of their time in compiling the list of players selected in this book. My thanks to all for their perseverance in narrowing down the final selection. In particular, I am grateful to Donal Cullinane from Cork and Jerry O'Sullivan from Cloyne in County Cork, who unfailingly made themselves available with advice. Both have a great feel for the game and are keen judges of the players who played throughout the ages. Likewise, Paddy Glackin of RTÉ, who has extensive knowledge of Gaelic football, was a huge help in the selection process, as was Dan Cullinane from Delanys in Cork.

I am particularly grateful to Ned Keane from Villierstown, County Waterford, whose feel for the sport and whose familiarity with the players helped steer me in the right direction. William 'Nooche' Kenefick, who comes from Youghal in County Cork, never flagged in his enthusiasm and support, was always available with advice and offered sound judgements of the players and their contributions to the game. Few know their sport quite like Ned or 'Nooche' and my gratitude extends to both.

The original inspiration for *Gaelic Football's Top 20* came from Ed Mulhall, Director of News in RTÉ, who suggested that I should write the book following the publication of *Hurling's Top 20*. Ed has always been full of enthusiasm and encouragement, for which I am genuinely grateful. Adrian Moynes, Managing Director, RTÉ Radio, supported the idea from the beginning, gave the all-clear to the accompanying radio programmes and allowed me the space and time to complete the project. Eithne Hand, Tom McGuire and Lorelei Harris also added their support. To all, I am grateful.

Within RTÉ, Fionnuala Hayes worked under pressure and transcribed the interviews with her usual care and concern. She also undertook some valuable and necessary research. That she did so with such good humour is a tribute to her character and her high professional standards. Noel Roberts, as always, brought his skills to bear on the radio programmes, mixing and balancing the sound with his usual diligence. Carolyn, Andrew and Lorraine Roberts often bore the brunt of Noel's dedication and my gratitude to them for their patience.

My thanks to Norman from Inpho, who helped with the photographic illustrations including the front cover. My gratitude to Billy Stickland from Inpho, who took many of the photos used in the book. Leo Gray from *The Sligo Champion*, Peter Thursfield from *The Irish Times* and Stan Shields from *The Connacht Tribune* also provided help. I am grateful to Barbara, Pauline, Rob, Joan and Ian from various RTÉ archives and libraries, and also Pearl Quinn from the RTÉ Stills Library. Bill Campbell, Peter MacKenzie and all the staff at Mainstream Publishing were a pleasure to work with, especially Tina,

INTRODUCTION

Ailsa, Elaine, Graeme, Fiona, Becky and Sharon, as well as Lorraine McCann. In addition, Anne Farrell of RTÉ, Dr Ernán Gallagher and Dr Seán Keane were especially supportive.

I am indebted to National University of Ireland, Maynooth, where President, Dr W. J. Smyth and Vice-President, Dr Frank Mulligan, the latter of whom played for Kildare, were generous in their support. The project also helped re-establish contacts with Fr Columba O'Donnell O.S.A. and Fr Anthony Hourihane O.S.A. Unfortunately, Fr Hourihane, who was a huge fan of Gaelic football and hurling, passed away before the book and radio series came to fruition. Above all, no list would be complete without Úna O'Hagan, who read the manuscript page by page and offered her comments and corrections, and also my son Seán Keane, whose involvement with Bray Emmets U-16s provided the initial spur for the book to be written. Without their co-operation and support the project would never have been finished.

Finally, to all those stars from all those teams who appear in the following pages, my gratitude for telling me their stories. Some were fortunate to play with great sides that were destined for multiple championship success. Others plied their trade year after year, doggedly turning up for training and matches in the drenching rain and bitter cold yet never tasting victory. For players like Sligo's Mickey Kearins and Mayo's Willie Joe Padden, the pain of missing out on a championship medal is all too plain to see. For others, like Mikey Sheehy and Pat Spillane, there's a record haul of eight All-Ireland senior medals to look back on now that their careers are over. Gaelic football is sometimes a cruel game. But it's never dull, that's for sure, as the first-hand testimonies in the following pages reveal.

Colm Keane
August 2003

1. SEÁN PURCELL

THEY WERE KNOWN AS 'THE TERRIBLE TWINS', WHICH WAS A PHRASE REPUTEDLY coined by the late Mick Dunne during his newspaper days. The players in question were Galway's Seán Purcell and Frank Stockwell. They both came from Tuam. They went to school together during their early years. They played minor together and progressed through senior ranks side by side. Both played with the famous Tuam Stars. They shared in Galway's senior All-Ireland success over Cork in 1956. And they developed an uncanny, almost telepathic understanding that terrorised defences from all corners of Ireland.

Frank Stockwell was the deadly sharpshooter who dazzled defences, a man who scored 2–5 in the 1956 All-Ireland decider, which is a record for a 60-minute final. Tucked in behind him was Seán Purcell, the master craftsman and magical conjurer who cast his spell on all he surveyed and who was selected on the Team of the Century and the Team of the Millennium. Arguably the finest footballer ever to grace the game, Purcell was a brilliant, natural, inspirational and versatile player who was comfortable in every position from the backs right through to the forwards. With the modest Purcell pulling the strings and Stockwell releasing the arrows, Galway were as effective as any football team could ever be.

'We were in babies school together in the Presentation and we were friends,' Seán Purcell recalls. 'Frank, of course, was a wonderful footballer. He was a wonderful athlete. I think any sport he took up he would excel at it. He was a fine boxer, a billiards player and a snooker player. He was magic with any kind of ball. As well as that, he had a tremendous spring. He could go as high off the ground as any man I've ever seen. Even though he wasn't a big man he was tremendously strong and, of course, he was a great poacher of scores. Unfortunately, he had many injuries in his career, which curtailed him quite a lot.

'Frank was a great ball-player, a great soloist, great at anything like that. He was an all-round, brilliant footballer and he would have been a great soccer player. He knew the simple things of the game, especially to pass. I'd give it to him and he'd give it back to me, or vice versa. We knew how to pass the ball to one another and give each other room to move and work the old one-twos. I'd give it to him so that he could move to get it and sometimes he would give me the ball back. We knew each other's play and where we might be and we could find each other well enough. It was a natural knowledge of each other's game and each other's strengths and weaknesses. In that way, we managed to put up the scores.

'It's a simple game really. If you give the ball to somebody, the best way that he can get it is if you don't pass when he has two or three men marking him. You give it to him so that he can run and move to get it himself. Frank would know that you were going to put the ball in a particular place. He would sense that. There was nothing made up about it. It was natural skill, if you like, on Frank's part anyway. We had a natural kind of empathy with each other and it worked out well. We managed to click together. There was nothing too organised about it. We just took it naturally.

'I always tried to get the ball and part with it to the best of my ability, whether to score or to give it to somebody in a better position. I suppose I was lucky to have a good sense of anticipation. I remember when I was a young lad in the college we used to have a couple of hours free after school and we'd be kicking the ball around. There would be a great crowd out on the field and you had to be very lucky or very good to get a kick at the ball. It would certainly improve your anticipation. You'd nearly know where everybody was going to kick it. You had to if you were going to get a kick at it yourself.

'In '56 Frank scored 2–5 in the final and with all respects to Jimmy Keaveney, who is a great friend of mine and who scored 2–6 in a 70-minute final, Frank's record lasts over a 60-minute game. They were all off his foot, no frees, 'twas a wonderful score and he was a wonderful striker. He destroyed the Cork defence on his own. It was just a matter of getting the ball in to him the best way we could. We tried the old tricks we had worked on over the years.

Things were much less scientific, I suppose, than they are now. We all contributed to each other but we knew Frank was the man to give the ball to and he'd do the rest.'

The senior career of Seán Purcell couldn't have begun at a more inauspicious time. Arriving on the Galway senior team in the late 1940s, he was just in time to witness the golden era of Mayo, who were Galway's great rivals in Connacht. Winners of four consecutive Connacht titles from 1948 to 1951, that Mayo team powered their way to two All-Ireland successes in 1950 and 1951. Boasting great players like captain Seán Flanagan, Paddy Prendergast, Tom Langan and Pádraig Carney, Mayo fought many great battles with their neighbours Galway. There were titanic battles between Seán Purcell and his Mayo opponents. Unfortunately, Mayo's success brought football famine for rising young stars like Galway's Seán Purcell.

'In the early 1950s, in '50 and '51, Mayo had a wonderful team,' Seán recollects. 'They won two All-Irelands and they overshadowed us for years. I remember one day they beat us very badly in Tuam. I happened to be in Galway that night and I met a great old friend of mine, a great footballer called Tom Langan. Tom was a very quiet man who didn't have much to say. But he had a few pints that night and he came over to me and he said: "Don't let that worry you. I played in six Connacht finals before I won one." Tom was a great footballer and a great man.

'We had been going through a bad time. We played Mayo in the Connacht final of 1948. There were two drawn games and they beat us in extra time. I remember those games very well. Our star was Tom Sullivan. I'd say that on his day he had to be the greatest one-man team of all time. Frank Stockwell was playing along with another great friend of mine, Jarlath Canavan, who had been unlucky enough to lose three All-Ireland finals in the early 1940s. I think Mayo were just coming right for that great team of theirs of the 1950s. After the '48 Connacht final, things went downhill for us. We kept playing and plugging away in the early 1950s. We didn't have a great team. We did have a few great games with Dublin in the league and Dublin at that time were the best team in Ireland. They had a tremendous team based on the St Vincent's team. They had Kevin Heffernan and Ollie Freaney. When they did win the All-Ireland I think Vincent's provided 13 or 14 of the team.

'Finally, I suppose, Mayo came to the end of their tether and we just happened to get lucky. It wasn't until '54 that we really made a breakthrough when we beat Mayo in the Connacht championship. Jack Mahon and myself said we were going to come good at some stage or the other. I remember meeting him before the '54 match with Mayo and we decided we had to give it everything, that we had a chance. We beat them against all the odds and after that then we took off. From there on, things fell into position easily enough.'

The rise of Galway in 1954 coincided with the almost total collapse of their great rivals Mayo. In '54 Seán Purcell won his first Connacht senior medal. In the next six years he added a further five to his medal collection. To begin with he played centre-field. He then moved to the backs, where he excelled in many great contests with his provincial rivals. Soon, however, he was moved up the field, where he settled in at centre-forward throughout Galway's great years. It was a tribute to his natural versatility and talent that the changes of position were effected with the greatest of ease.

'I enjoyed the game and had to fit in here and there at different times,' Seán says. 'We had a great club in Tuam that time and we had plenty of football so we played around the place. Things weren't as specialised as they are now. I probably started off centre-field and moved towards the backs. In '54 I was full-back and then I went to centre-forward, where myself and Frank Stockwell had a great knowledge of each other's game. Frank was a very experienced footballer at that time and I was too. We just managed to click together. There was nothing too organised about it. We just took it naturally.'

The pinnacle of Galway's revival was reached on 7 October 1956 at Dublin's Croke Park. Some two years before, Galway had experienced defeat by Kerry at the semi-final stage of the championship. This time there would be no repeat of that failure. Having waited patiently for the final to take place, which was delayed due to Cork's tragic polio epidemic, Galway took their chance with vigour and style. That was the day Seán Purcell and Frank Stockwell wove their magic spell. With Purcell orchestrating the show, Stockwell pounded the Cork defence into submission. The unselfish Purcell repeatedly fed the hungry Stockwell, who slammed a record 2–5 past the hapless Cork defence. That record remains intact for a 60-minute final, although Jimmy Keaveney later surpassed it in 1977 in a 70-minute final. The final score in the 1956 decider: Galway 2–13, Cork 3–7.

'Frank was unbeatable that day,' Seán recalls. 'He really went to town. He scored a couple of goals and five points. He foraged for himself to a great extent. He destroyed the Cork defence on his own. It was just a matter of getting the ball in to him the best way we could. I think he had most of it scored by half-time. We had a great lead at half-time and Cork came back at us in a big way. They really put it up to us and they got back to within a point or so. We were lucky enough to get back one or two points at the end.

'We got a wonderful reception at home. I remember that quite well, coming from Dublin into Tuam. By present day standards the crowds wouldn't be the same but it was a great night in Tuam. The match would have been broadcast around the town all day and there would have been a great spirit of victory around the place. When we arrived in Tuam I think the crowd met us and we were carried shoulder-high or on the lorry down to the town. We had a meal somewhere and there was speechmaking.

'We were fêted in every town and village in the county. You know how it goes on in the present day but we did it in our own time in the 1950s. It was wonderful to go to all the towns in the county with the cup, be fêted, have a meal and so on. You can imagine all the excitement it created in all the small towns we went to and in the schools where we visited with the cup. I have very pleasant memories of that. The feeling was one of great joy and happiness having won the All-Ireland at last after so many years.'

In 1957 Galway worked their way through Connacht to the All-Ireland semi-final, where they again faced Cork. This time, however, Cork exacted revenge over the champions and Galway's dreams of two titles in succession were shattered. The Tribesmen also lost to Dublin in the 1958 championship semi-final. However, they did achieve some consolation with a National Football League title in 1957, winning for Seán Purcell the only league medal of his career. For the record, that league victory was secured with a 1–8 to 0–7 victory over Kerry.

'We had a very good final against Kerry,' Seán says. 'I was in full-forward trying to draw out the full-back, Ned Roche. We were moving out towards the sideline and I saw Frank moving in. I managed to get a ball across to him, to where he came in. He met it and punched it into the net. It was the winning goal. Then we had to play in New York. I remember that too because many of our lads got sick over there. New York had a fine team at the time. The GAA was very strong in New York in the 1950s. We played them in the Polo Grounds and we managed to win that too. It was a very good game.'

Galway's momentum carried them to a further All-Ireland final in 1959, where they faced a Kerry team captained by the great Mick O'Connell. The opposing captain that day was Seán Purcell. It was the young O'Connell's first All-Ireland final. In sharp contrast, Seán Purcell was a veteran of the game with All-Ireland, National Football League and a bundle of provincial titles under his belt. Unfortunately for Galway, the magic of Purcell and Stockwell failed to materialise on the day and Kerry romped home by 3–7 to 1–4.

'I think I made a rather stupid mistake early on,' Seán recalls of that 1959 final. 'I was playing full-forward. Niall Sheehy was a big strong man and the ball was going wide. I could have left it go but I saw Niall coming towards me. I said I'd get my retaliation in first and I did. I hit him an almighty crack with my forearm across the head and he got in under me and he put me up in the air. I really thought I had killed him but when I looked up all he did was shake his head a few times and trot away. It was a bad start, a foolish mistake and after that we were well beaten. We didn't really make much of a show. The lads did their best all right but we just weren't good enough that day.'

By the close of the 1950s Seán Purcell also had accumulated three Railway Cup medals won with Connacht in 1951, '57 and '58. In each of those Railway Cup finals they beat Munster. Connacht narrowly won by a point in 1951. They won by a more convincing six points in 1957. They virtually repeated the performance in 1958, when they ran out winners by a margin of five points. It was a remarkable haul for a province that effectively faced the might of a Munster side dominated by Kerry and Cork, incorporating at various times stars like Paddy Bawn Brosnan and Mick O'Connell.

'It was a great honour to play for Connacht,' Seán remarks. 'There wouldn't be any specialised training. We'd always do a bit of training on our own. It was early in the year and we had to get the turkey out of our system. We always did a little bit for it and we had a fine team. You had at that time the nucleus of the great Mayo team, with Flanagan, Prendergast, Dixon and Carney. We had Gerry O'Malley from Roscommon, who was a great footballer. We had Nace O'Dowd from Sligo and, of course, Packie McGarty, who was nearly a one-man team himself. He was a great footballer.

'We got on very well together and we were lucky to win three of the things. The crowd in Croke Park for the final on St Patrick's Day would always be around 40,000 to 50,000 and you'd have the cream of the Munster hurlers there. The great Christy Ring would always put on a magic display in the Railway Cup finals. He had 18 medals and we used to really love watching him perform. The crowds really enjoyed it. When the club championships were initiated I think the spirit went out of the Railway Cups. I would hate to see them go altogether. They were great in my time.'

Witnesses to Seán Purcell's football ability testify to the style, skill and command of a game that great legends possess. Many of those witnesses, some of them great footballers themselves, argue that the completeness and diversity of his talents mark him out as the finest footballer of all time. His ability to play at the highest level in any part of the field is a rare quality in football. His intuitive instincts and natural flair were certainly unique. Almost as impressive was his unselfish willingness to commit his skills to the good of the team, in particular by acting as provider to one of the other great Galway stars, Frank Stockwell.

Following his retirement Seán Purcell was recognised as something of an elder statesman and ambassador of the game, appearing at many awards ceremonies where he was honoured for his contribution to football. Adding to his single senior All-Ireland, one National Football League, six Connacht championships and the huge number of medals won with Tuam Stars, he was also in receipt of some of the game's highest awards. In 1984 he was voted on to the Team of the Century and in 1999 he was selected on the Team of the Millennium, both awards marking the culmination of a playing career that began in the late 1940s and that came to a close in the early 1960s.

'We had one last crack at it in '60,' Seán concludes. 'We got to the

All-Ireland semi-final but Kerry beat us again. I don't remember anything very much about that semi-final but I think we were beginning to fade. I played on for another season or two and my final game came in Castlebar in 1962. We were winning comfortably against Roscommon when the crossbar broke. By the time it was fixed Gerry O'Malley took over and he ran riot. He set up two goals and we were beaten. It was my last game for Galway, in the championship anyway.

'I have many great friends and it's lovely to meet them. We have our memories. It's a great thing to meet the lads now and again and share those few memories. May the Lord have mercy on all the lads that are gone. Quite a few of the lads I played with have passed on. But it's nice to be remembered and the awards are all right. Whether I deserved some of them or not is another question.'

2. MICK O'CONNELL

SHORTLY AFTER MICK O'CONNELL COLLECTED THE SAM MAGUIRE CUP IN 1959, HE
headed home to Kerry. It was a long trip to Valentia Island. He
travelled by train into the Kerry night. He then rowed his boat to the
O'Connell family home on the island. It was Mick's first All-Ireland
final. He had captained Kerry that day. Behind him in Dublin, the
Kerry fans and players celebrated into the autumn darkness. This,
after all, was a celebration of Kerry's league and championship
double. For Mick O'Connell, however, the job was done. Kerry had
won and there was work to be attended to the following day.

That September day in 1959, Kerry had beaten Galway to win
their nineteenth championship title. Wonderful players lined out in
the green and gold. There was Tadhgie Lyne, Tom Long and Mick
O'Dwyer. There was the great Seán Murphy and Johnny Culloty in
goal. But no player would subsequently outshine the young
midfielder unveiled on the football stage that day. It wasn't his finest
game; he was sick before the match and came off injured. Yet
national audiences had just witnessed the arrival of one of football's
finest exponents and greatest legends, the Team of the Century and
Team of the Millennium midfielder, Mick O'Connell.

'I was playing pretty well at that time,' Mick recalls. 'I played with
the South Kerry team and we won the Kerry county championship
three years in a row. Then I was selected as Kerry captain in '59 and
I was playing for a few years at that time. It would always be nice to
look forward to your first All-Ireland and a young lad likes to prove
himself that he is capable of being up there with the best. That final,
in particular, should have been probably the most memorable, but it
wasn't one of the most satisfying because the week beforehand I got
a lot of wettings and colds going across to practice.

21

'I had a hell of a sore throat the weekend of the match. My throat was sealed with the soreness and you cannot play well then. But there's no pulling out on the morning of the match because it's assumed that you're letting the side down. Dr Éamonn O'Sullivan gave me some tablets on the morning of the match but it was too late then. I couldn't swallow a spit. A man, unless he's in good form, cannot play well and I'm not making any excuses for that. It happened to many others and to myself other times as well. On the day, because of ill-feeling or something like that, the ball may not run your way even when you're in the height of form and when you've trained and you're as fit as can be.

'During the game I happened to twist my knee as well and the Galway lads probably had the upper hand at midfield. People are often castigated because they don't play well on a particular day. I didn't have a good game that day but you must judge a person over a period. Coming back that night was always my practice. I'd play a match, have my meal or whatever with the team and come home. It was no different in the case of that final. To think that you should gallivant around the city and be proclaiming yourself as champions, that was never my style. In fact, the ceremony attached to the game, this parading around and this posturing before the match started, was never very attractive to me. I would enjoy a game in Cahirciveen or Valentia or Tralee as much as an All-Ireland, often more so because those trimmings and waiting around for the match to start before an All-Ireland meant nothing to me really.

'I worked with the Western Union Cable Company on the island and all the other workers were at work early on Monday morning. Why should I, because of my sport or pastime, get exception for that? I wouldn't expect it or I wouldn't ask it either. That was the ethos at that time. Nowadays, it seems that you're supposed to be celebrating and you get time off from your job. Yet, on the other hand, I hear people say they're making sacrifices. For myself personally, my first All-Ireland could have been more satisfying if I had been in top form and played well. But looking back on it now, I've no disappointments. It was won by Kerry and that was reasonably satisfying.'

Mick O'Connell grew up in the 1940s and '50s in an era when Gaelic football was very different from the modern game. Born on

Valentia Island in 1937, he arrived at a time when the skills of 'catch and kick' dominated the sport. This was the era of great fielders and kickers of the ball. It was also, of course, a time when legendary Kerry teams won all before them, securing All-Ireland titles not alone in the year of Mick's birth but also a famous three-in-a-row from 1939 to 1941 and further titles in 1946, 1953 and 1955. Great players like Paddy Bawn Brosnan and Jackie Lyne graced the game. Inevitably, on the fields of Valentia Island Mick O'Connell emulated their skills and talents.

'The game I came into was a game of catch the ball, kick the ball and one of the big things was the struggle to win the 50-50 ball,' Mick recollects. 'I never saw a solo run, I'd say, until the early 1950s and it seems strange nowadays, half a century later, to say that. I suppose various players get a kick out of sport in different ways, but I thought the one thing that was unique to Gaelic football, which is almost extinct now, is the high catch. That's the ball delivered down the field and it's a challenge to oneself to get up there and catch it at full-stretch even if there's no opponent present. That was something that appealed to me.

'I got satisfaction from being able to catch well and kick well, and I suppose anything you do fairly well if you are fairly competent at it you get more enjoyment from it. I remember in recent years I was talking to a young lad who didn't do so very well in competition and I said: "You didn't seem to practise very much." "Ah, no," he said, "we were only in it for the *craic*." My response to that was: "Sure, we were all in it for the *craic* but the *craic* is much more fulfilling and enjoyable if you're fairly good at it." That is the way I would still look at it, that you'll get as much out of it as you put into it. I put a fair bit into it.

'When I was growing up on Valentia Island, my people were seagoing people and most of my time was spent either doing work on the small farm we had or on the fishing boats. Kicking the ball was done with the schoolboys around in the field at home. There was no such thing as an organised game. We played our own game and enjoyed playing with the ball, which seems far away from the U-10, U-12 and U-14 competitions now. There was no such thing in those times as training or practice. We just played football and in my particular time I happened to like it and I happened to get fairly good at it.

'There were no ambitions that you would be playing for a county or anything like that. It wasn't the culture of the household or of the area. People at that time went to national school; probably a few went on to secondary school and nobody at all to third level. For that reason, many good, talented young lads grew up and went away to England and other places and never got a chance. I happened to get an opportunity to stay on the island and get a job during my football years. That's how I happened to be in it.'

In 1955 Mick O'Connell won his first county championship medal as the youngest player on the South Kerry team. In May of that year he also played his first game in Kerry colours, togging out at midfield for the county minors. Within 12 months he had progressed to the Kerry senior team, where he made his début against Cork at the Cork Athletic Grounds in May 1956. Almost overnight he was on his way to play in New York. Selected at midfield, the senior inter-county career of Mick O'Connell had taken off.

Up to 1959 the Kerry senior team failed to set the world of football on fire. They lost the 1956 Munster final to Cork, got knocked out of the championship by Waterford in 1957 and were defeated by Derry in the All-Ireland semi-final in 1958. Progress, however, was steadily being made and in 1959 the team landed the double of National Football League and All-Ireland championship. These were the growing years for Mick O'Connell, a time when he learned the finer points of the game, honed his skills, fine-tuned his fitness, practised his fielding and kicking and relished every moment of his involvement in football.

'It was enjoyable,' Mick reflects. 'I suppose when a person is young and coming out of the teenage years and young manhood, you'd like to prove yourself. They are carefree days of youth. There are no other commitments. Nothing ever crosses your mind about settling down or anything else. That was the way I felt about it anyway. You were as free as the wind to practise and you were interfering with nobody else's life. It was great to feel good and fit in those years and it was something that was very fulfilling because you were involved in something that was exciting and that was apart from the ordinary job of earning a living.

'It was nice to have a weekend away to look forward to, especially living in a place on the west coast. I wouldn't have seen Dublin very much, and maybe other places as well, except on the day of a match. I saw many parts of Ireland through it, and during the week I enjoyed practising. I suppose 95 per cent of the practising was done on the island. I practised myself. I had a field at the back of the house and I did a lot of exercising and running there. I didn't have great facilities and it was a fair struggle. But often when the struggle is there it makes it more satisfying in that you can overcome those difficulties. That's maybe why for me it was fairly fulfilling.

'There was always a good tradition of football on Valentia Island and young and not so young and often old fellows would always rally around and kick the ball to me. You can be good at some sports but in Gaelic football you need the ball driven to you to practise fielding and to keep your eye in. I got the alliance of many a person, neighbours and people passing by the road, sometimes light-keepers who'd be on shore for a while and people like that. A lot of them were rounded up to give me some practise. On the whole, I was privileged that there was a tradition of football on Valentia. Only for that, if this island happened to be off the coast of Clare or somewhere else, there would never be a mention of me.'

By the time Mick O'Connell won his second All-Ireland medal in 1962, he was already a giant of the game. He was, by then, renowned for his majestic fielding of the ball and his pinpoint kicking with both feet. Possessing balance and vision, he could judge the flight and pace of the ball to perfection. No one could touch the sky quite like O'Connell, catching balls with uncanny timing and sending accurate shots either over the bar or to his fellow-players. Words like grace and style were used to describe this unique Kerry midfielder who, like Christy Ring in hurling, stood out among his peers.

'My unique style was to stay back and take a run and get off the ground,' Mick says. 'Obstructionist tactics were often used where people drifted across my path. Some people would say: "Watch his line of run and obstruct." It wouldn't be observed by a referee or by people on the sideline. That negative thing was never part of my game and I cannot understand how true-blue amateurs go out to play and just have obstructionist tactics like that instead of doing the best they can. I've played many a game myself and if people beat me to a ball, so be it. You win one and you might lose one, but overall if the flow of the game is there you'll get your chance as well.'

Throughout the 1960s Mick O'Connell and Kerry had ample opportunity to display their skills at national level. This was the era of mass audiences following Telefís Éireann's arrival in 1962. That year Kerry beat Roscommon in the first televised final. The following year Kerry lost the championship semi-final to Galway. In 1964 they again lost to Galway but this time in the All-Ireland final. Another defeat by Galway in the 1965 championship final was followed by a loss to Down in the 1968 decider. With victory over Offaly secured at last in the 1969 All-Ireland final, it seemed that Kerry and Mick O'Connell were seldom off our television screens. Whether the national broadcaster was televising Kerry's championship battles or their National Football League successes, the image of midfielder Mick O'Connell in the thick of battle will remain forever with the 1960s generation.

'I think the National Football League final in 1961 was where I was at my supreme best in fielding,' Mick says. 'It wasn't a very demanding game because we won it easily. That particular day I caught everything that I went for, which is a great feeling, to get off the ground and to catch some good balls like that. My most satisfying years were between, say, '55 and '65 when I was playing with Kerry. In '66 the job I had closed down and I went to England for a year. I didn't play at all in '67. I came back at the end of the 1960s and played into the early 1970s.

'At that time, television had come into it and the game was evolving. There was a bit more solo running and hand passing, well not hand passing but fist passing. The short game seemed to be coming into it more. I would be all for the short game provided it is aligned to the long game but not when it's passing a few yards to each other. Looking back on it, it was one of the mistakes I made. I think when I finished in '66 I should have stayed out. I came back and I played a number of years, I got about five pretty good years out of it and was still fairly fit. But the period in life as an amateur between the ages of 17 or 18 and coming on to the 30s was the most enjoyable time of my football days.'

In 1970 Kerry won a further All-Ireland title by defeating Meath. With that victory Mick O'Connell won his fourth All-Ireland medal. It was achieved as the player touched on his third decade in championship football. By now, the game was changing more than ever before. The influence of Australian football, which was first brought to Ireland in the late 1960s, was beginning to be felt. A faster, running game, which many felt was closer to the game of basketball than the traditional catch and kick game of Gaelic football, was about to come to the fore. There was soloing and hand passing. There were so many changes in train, including the arrival of a more professional approach to the game.

'I knew there were certain little things that could be improved,' Mick reflects. 'The Kerry team in my time wouldn't bring a football on to the field before a match and to warm up before the match and to practise a bit of fielding and kicking because it was reckoned to be ostentatious and to show off. Regarding a masseur, I had a good masseur who gave me wonderful service. I thought any county team at the time should have a full-time masseur, not treating injuries but getting the muscles right so that everybody would be fluid and loose on the day. A little bit of professionalism in an amateur code wouldn't cost very much but it would enhance the fitness of players and their feeling for the game.

'It brings to mind how in the 2002 World Cup Roy Keane was castigated right, left and centre for wanting high standards. He was captain of Manchester United, going out to Japan, and there wasn't a training ground, there wasn't football gear and they were running barbecues for the media, trimmings that had nothing to do with producing a better player on the field. He rebelled against it and for that reason he was blackened right, left and centre. I think the man was right to look for high standards. Talking about our own code, as an amateur code Gaelic was great fun and we enjoyed it. But the fun is much better if everything is organised in a semi-professional manner and if everything is right. If players are in good form, they're going to perform better.

'As regards changes in the actual code itself, I've given up on that because, as I've hinted down through the years, even players who are now old-timers like myself will always revert back to the parochial. Will Kerry beat Cork? Will Dublin beat Meath? The will to win is grand in its own way but not at the price of the game. In the last half-century the game has changed but I don't know if it has improved. Many times through the years all the administrators knew that there was something wrong with the game, that it wasn't as good as it might be. They tried this and they tried that without any conviction about what they wanted. They said that change is good. I've heard time after time that change is good. In my opinion, the way the game of Gaelic football has evolved is that the trimmings, the solo run, the hand passing, are the main course. Fielding and good kicking seem to be secondary to that. I think the reverse should be the order.

'If you talk about win-at-all-costs, I suppose any team that trains for a match wants to win but again the players at the present time have come up with an ethos in Gaelic which is that the foul is acceptable. The referees have an impossible job because there's foul after foul. If they whistled all the fouls that are there, it would be non-stop use of the whistle. I'd say the players are often ignorant of the actual rules and I'd say the way the play has been allowed to develop has encouraged that. The running with the ball, charging with the ball and the pulling and dragging are things I would like to say something about but I know it's pointless. It is up to the administration but I think they haven't the vision to tackle the problem.

'I'm longer involved in the game than most people in life today. I met men who were in America in the 1930s and they said that the Kerry team that went out to New York in the late '20s and early '30s were the finest team of traditional Gaelic footballers that they ever saw. They won several All-Irelands but they're gone into obscurity now. Yet in recent years we're talking about "the greatest player" or "the greatest team". I think that depends on what you're talking about, you're not comparing like with like. I would think it's much easier to play or to practise the more modern game if you can run and if you can learn a bit of hand passing. I think it's much more challenging to develop high fielding, good two-footed kicking, and I think that was the part of the game that should have been developed. Mobility and speed will add to any game but not if the other side of the game is being neglected.'

While obviously a keen student of Gaelic football, Mick O'Connell also took an avid lifelong interest in other sports, especially hurling, rugby and soccer. As it happened, however, it was the unlikely sport of American football that Mick almost played in the early 1970s. That close encounter with the oval ball happened in

1973 when John Kerry O'Donnell, the New York GAA administrator, invited Mick and a party of other Irish sportsmen on a trip to Los Angeles. There he was introduced to Jack Faulkner of the Los Angeles Rams, who was impressed with Mick's credentials. Although initial contract moves were instigated, Mick's unlikely transfer from Valentia Island to Los Angeles never materialised.

'I was finished playing,' Mick remarks. 'I was on a trip out in the Pacific. Ollie Walsh, Niall Sheehy and Christy Ring were on the same trip and I got to meet the Los Angeles side. I did some kicking there and they were talking about coming out and doing a trial. I was 36 and newly-married and I couldn't risk it. But I know well that in my earlier times if I got the proper boot and proper kick, I could have kicked that ball pretty well. It would be nice to have sampled it. As you see on television, you've only seconds to get the kick off with maybe 20 men coming at speed down on you. To play a game at the highest level, it's only then you can be at your very best. It's something that I often thought about. It must be a great feeling for a person who has done that. I never got the chance to do it, but again I have no regrets.'

By the time he had finished playing in the mid-1970s, Mick O'Connell had tasted victory in four senior All-Irelands, six National Football Leagues and 12 Munster Senior Football Championships. He also had amassed a vast haul of divisional and county championship medals. He was Footballer of the Year in 1962 and he was later selected on both the Team of the Century and the Team of the Millennium. However, it isn't for the medals or awards that Mick O'Connell is remembered. Wherever fans and critics gather, they compare him with supreme legends from other sports whose attributes of dedication, skill, ability and passion mark them out as a cut above the rest.

'I have good memories,' Mick concludes. 'Many of the people who were mentors or players are long departed. In fact, there are about eight of the 1962 All-Ireland team now deceased, sad to say. But I'm still there. That period of my life I enjoyed and I'm thankful for it, although by no means was it everything. It doesn't absorb me that much now as I'm 30 years gone from the game. I still have an interest in all sports and I think playing Gaelic football is what gave me the interest.

'I think sport is a great common denominator. No matter where you go you can bring up a discussion on sport and that's what interests me as much as the actual winning and losing. Even as I speak now, I would still go for a kick-around just for fun if I got people like Maurice Fitzgerald with his father Ned and my special son Diarmuid in the yard down below. I wouldn't be able to play a match or anything like that. That feeling you get from just a few kicks of the ball is wonderful. I see a lot of other old players in other sports who play tennis or something else like golf. I would enjoy a few kicks of the ball like that. It gives an old-timer the feel of the game once again.'

3. SEÁN O'NEILL

WITH THE BATTLE-CRY OF 'REMEMBER LISTOWEL', THE DOWN FOOTBALLERS CHARGED
onto the pitch at Croke Park on 25 September 1960 to face Kerry in
the All-Ireland final. Down were going for what would be their very
first championship title and the first for any team from the Six
Counties. Kerry were vying for their twentieth championship crown
and their second All-Ireland in succession. Kerry boasted star names
like Mick O'Connell, Mick O'Dwyer, Tom Long, Johnny Culloty and
Tadhgie Lyne. Down, at that stage, were virtual unknowns, although
players like Paddy Doherty, James and Dan McCartan, Joe Lennon
and Seán O'Neill would soon become household names.

That the final had its own inbuilt tensions and passions was
beyond dispute. In the months preceding the contest a strange
alchemy had strained relations between the men from Kerry and the
men from Down. Perhaps it all started to go wrong when the upstarts
from Ulster had beaten league champions Kerry in the National
Football League semi-final and gone on to claim the 1960 league
title. Not amused by this slight, Kerry had exacted revenge on Down
during a so-called 'friendly' staged in Listowel. Scarred by the
experience of a resounding defeat, the Down players ran onto Croke
Park with a message for the men from the Kingdom.

'It was an innocuous challenge match played in Listowel,' Seán
O'Neill recalls of that 'friendly' in County Kerry. 'The Down side were
invited to open the pitch in Listowel before the championship
started. We went down and it was a weekend of fun and relaxation.
The management of the team decided: "Look, you need a break, the
whip's off, enjoy your weekend." That's exactly what we went down
to do. We had a marvellous weekend in Listowel and some of the
boys weren't in bed until four o'clock in the morning. The following

morning some of them were away to Tralee and arrived back just a few minutes before the game in Listowel. There was no pressure.

'Unfortunately, we met a Kerry team who were bent on correcting the defeat in the league semi-final and they really played at championship pitch that day. We were totally unprepared for that and they beat us by about 15 or 16 points, as I recall. I was injured. I wasn't playing in the game and I was along the sideline. They were leading by about 12 points with about 10 or 15 minutes to go. I can remember John Dowling, who was a great player and a marvellous man, saying: "Send the ball in low, lads, it's goals we want." In a challenge match that was not on and it was a big mistake.

'We lost the match but we said afterwards that Kerry made a very major mistake because they really went out to teach us a lesson and they did. We learnt the lesson. That came back to haunt them because one of the last comments that we made on leaving the dressing-room before the 1960 All-Ireland final, when we were going out onto Croke Park, was: "Remember Listowel". That was a big motivator in the back of our heads. Our pride was hurt and we thought that Kerry had stolen a march on us. We were upstarts from the North and I'm sure that Kerry with their great tradition thought it was time that Down were put in their place. Listowel was as good as any place to do it. As it turned out, we read that to suit ourselves and I'm not sure if Kerry understood that we were reading it that way.'

All-Ireland final day in 1960 introduced to national football audiences a fresh and youthful Down team full of inventive flair and playing an exhilarating brand of total football. Backed by a thorough and efficient backroom staff, the Down senior footballers were fast and skilful, exciting to watch and admired for their intelligent and refreshing style of play. Fresh out of Ulster, they were virtually unknown to southern crowds. In time, however, one of their forwards, Seán O'Neill, would make his mark not alone as Footballer of the Year but also by being selected on both the Team of the Century and the Team of the Millennium.

Although National Football League champions, Down arrived at Croke Park as underdogs to the reigning All-Ireland champions Kerry. Down had just won their very first national senior title by defeating Cavan in the league decider. They had progressed through

Ulster by defeating Cavan for the second time in a row in an Ulster final. They had squeezed past Offaly in the All-Ireland semi-final. Their fans arrived in droves at Croke Park to witness what they hoped would be a major piece of history. They were not to be disappointed as Down, managed by the great Barney Carr, defeated Kerry by 2–10 to 0–8, sending their supporters into a frenzy of excitement and securing the Sam Maguire Cup for a cross-border county for the very first time.

'This was a massive game,' Seán says. 'This was a history-in-the-making game. But the thing I can assure you of is that when we left the dressing-room that day, we had absolutely no fear of Kerry. We respected and admired them greatly but we had no fear of them. We were not afraid of that game. We were there to win. I'm not sure if Kerry understood the mentality of the Down side going out that day. We had beaten Kerry in the league. Kerry could argue logically that the league doesn't count, that the championship is a different matter altogether. But we had confidence. There was great confidence in the Down squad, which was often read as arrogance. For example, we burst onto the field that day in Croke Park; that was our keenness to get on the park. We had a job to do and we were there to do it.

'Kerry traditionally came out very slowly. They could even walk out at times. You'd sometimes wonder! The first time I saw a Kerry side I think was in '55. I was a youngster watching them against Cavan and they came out in ones and twos, they walked out of the dressing-room right onto the park. I'm looking at these people and saying: "Are they really interested in playing here today?" I didn't know a lot about them at that point but I knew of this great tradition they had and it amazed me that they came out in such a laconic way. When we hit the park it could have looked like arrogance but it wasn't that. Anybody who knows the Down players from that time knows they were not arrogant. They were absolutely rock-solid confident in their ability and we took the field that day in a confident frame of mind.

'We knew we had the measure of Kerry if we played our football. But you have to perform and the big thing was to perform and not to freeze, not to let the day get to you. It's thanks to the tremendous backroom team that we had that the team was mentally right to take on what was a very big assignment. You don't ever know going into a game if you're going to win or lose. But what you do know is that the only team that will beat you is the team that beats your best. If you go out in a major game like that and give your best, whatever that is, that's all that can be required of any player. We were determined to do it that day. We didn't know for sure what was going to happen and I don't think Kerry could have known either. But I think that Kerry probably felt that they were going to teach the whippersnappers from the North a lesson and that this was the time to do it. As it turned out, that did not happen.

'I don't think that you appreciate at the time what the achievement is. We were there to do a job; we were there to win a match. It was another match and a big match, but when you're involved at that level in competitive sport the winning of the game is what you are concentrating on, not what the historical effect of it is going to be. We were not concerned about being the first team to bring the cup across the border. That was a historical fact but it was not on our minds when we went to defeat Kerry. We were there to beat a great Kerry side on the field and we had to win many battles to do that. When the match is over, there's a fantastic sensation of relief that you've achieved something very special. We had won an All-Ireland championship and you cannot do better than that.

'When the historical significance of it and the impact of it came afterwards, you realised that it was a very historic win. At the time you don't analyse and assess your own team, but I look back now and I know that it was a great team. It had to be a great team because we had so many things to overcome, mental, physical, sporting, and the team had to win that first major All-Ireland. That is a very difficult task and a team has to be maybe twice as good to do it. The 1960 win was a very important breakthrough for the six northern counties because prior to that Cavan were the only other Ulster county to have won an All-Ireland championship and it was felt that the teams from the Six Counties always seemed to promise a lot and achieve nothing. The difference in attitude between the Down side of 1960 and other teams that had gone before was that we had total confidence in our ability and we were not afraid of any team. You must never be afraid to lose if you want to win. We weren't afraid to lose but we were determined not to lose. The difference was that we went to Dublin to win.'

In 1961 Down cruised through Ulster to win their third consecutive provincial title with victory over Armagh in the final. Kerry provided the opposition in the All-Ireland semi-final and they were dismissed by a score of 1–12 to 0–9. Back in the championship decider for the second year running, Down's opponents were Offaly. By now, the young Down team were evolving into a fast, fluent, tightly knit unit. They were high on confidence and self-belief following their remarkable breakthrough the previous year. Engulfed by a sea of red and black, they delivered another historic performance at Croke Park and defeated a great Offaly side by the narrow score of 3–6 to 2–8. Bringing with them their new thrilling brand of football, the Down players had taken the country by storm.

'I think every county has a natural style,' Seán observes. 'Kerry has a style, Dublin has a style, Galway has a style, Cork has a style, Derry has a style and Armagh has a style. All counties, in my view, have a style within their own club structures. Their club football is played in a certain way. Donegal play a very different kind of club football than would be played in Down, for example. Theirs is more of a short-passing, inter-marking, quick-running game. Our club game involves a long use of the ball. We play a longer game. The game that the Down senior team displayed as they progressed was really a reflection of what the club football was like in Down. That was a mix of a game, it was a mix of the short and the long.

'Contrary to what a lot of people think, the Down team was not a short-passing team. We did not believe in the short pass, we believed in the longer pass. We believed in making the ball do the travelling. Paddy Doherty, for example, could split a defence with a 40-yard ball in behind. It was devastating for defences because you can't defend that kind of ball. That's the kind of game that we were trying to play. It was a style that evolved, it wasn't manufactured, it suited the players that we had and reflected the way that football was played in the county. I think the style evolved with the team and we learned as we went along.

'My own role was the traditional role of a half-forward. There wasn't anything special or extraordinarily different in what I was expected to be doing. First of all, the duty of any forward is to be a scoring forward. Secondly, you're expected to defend when you have to defend and come back in and help out midfield or help out at the half-back line. We were a very fluid team, we were very fit and the fitness levels were very high at that time. I'd say we were easily the fittest team in Ireland at about February, March or April in any year. We were building on that then, you see. We were not losing ground and other teams were not overtaking us. Our fitness levels then were increasing in time for the championships.

'There were so many disparate kinds of talent on the team but they all came together into a unity. It was like the parts coming together to form a unity which was formidable. There's a certain point in the life of any great team when a group of players suddenly becomes a team and then they are formidable. This is when the sum of the parts, the unity of the parts, becomes so much greater. It's like a fusing. I used to compare it to an electrician connecting up an electrical board. You fuse it all together and suddenly the thing is strong. It's stronger than all the individual points. I think a team is like that. There's a point in the life of a team when fusion takes place. It's quite an extraordinary thing. From then on you're not dealing with individuals, you're dealing with a group. That's what we had. The reason that we were so successful is that we managed that fusion, which in essence was unselfish, committed performances to each other and a refusal to accept defeat.

'Another feature was that the Down management rarely arranged for us to play teams in challenge games that were not as good as us. We always played teams that were better than us and it was Maurice Hayes who had the very clear view that we had to meet southern teams. We had to meet teams from the west and from the south and from the east. We played challenge matches against Dublin, against Kerry, against teams like Galway. We were not meeting these teams in regular competition because in the league in Ulster you were confined to Ulster teams. There is a disadvantage there in that the only time you met these other major teams was in a very serious match in an All-Ireland semi-final and you were meeting them for the very first time.

'It was felt that it was better to go and meet these teams in friendly games because at least you got to know who they were. You got to know how they played, what style of football they played and you learned that they weren't supermen at all and that we could put our football up against any of them. It was a learning process. We could

learn from them. I think one of the great things about the Down team
was that we learned from our defeats and you must do that. If you're
to become a championship-winning team, you must learn from
every game that you play. I think we did that. We learned a lot from
Kerry. I certainly learned a lot from my games against Kerry over the
years. You learn how to be patient, you learn about adversity and
how to handle it. You learn how not to be put off by decisions that
went against you. Those are things a team gains by experience.

'You can never assess your own impact. I think it's quite a mystery
to a lot of Down people even yet what the impact of that team was
throughout the whole of Ireland. I'm not sure that we brought
anything all that different to the game. Journalists have said that we
brought something new and different. Whether it was the new team,
the new approach we had to the game, I just don't know. I'm sure
that the Dublin team of the 1950s brought something but our
football was a fairly traditional game, played at high speed by very
good players. The impact of the Down team on the public was
something we did not realise. It was just that the team had charisma
maybe, which we didn't understand ourselves, but I think it was
there all right.'

Throughout the remainder of the 1960s, Down added a further
four Ulster titles to their growing collection of honours. They
reached the All-Ireland semi-final in 1965 and 1966 but lost to
Galway and Meath respectively. In 1968 they faced Galway again at
the semi-final stage of the championship and this time reversed the
result. Back in an All-Ireland final for the third time that decade, it
was a new and relatively untried Down team that took to the field at
Croke Park. Seán O'Neill had by now moved to full-forward. He
scored one of the great All-Ireland final goals that day with a difficult
follow-through shot from a rebound off the woodwork. And who
else should Down beat in the 1968 decider other than their old
adversaries, Kerry! The final score that day: Down 2–12, Kerry 1–13.

'In '68 we started off with a very young team,' Seán recalls. 'There
were about seven or eight of the Down minor team that lost an All-
Ireland in 1966 in that squad. They were only two years out of minor
and were very young. The fusion took place in a drawn game with
Meath. Meath were All-Ireland champions and we played them once
in the league and we drew with them. We played them again early in

1968 and we beat them. Our young team had beaten the champions. Suddenly, this young team began to believe in themselves and they began to play with the fusion and the unity which is the mark of a great team and which a great team has to have. I knew there was something very special about this team and the fact that Meath had probably been on a bender from the previous October didn't register with us at all. We felt that we had beaten a good side and that's what started it for that team.

'The '68 squad relied very heavily on a very good tactical game and Gerry Brown, who was the manager of that side, was a master-tactician. He was a marvellous man in every way. His attitudes to the game were sporting, committed, courageous and skilful. Those were the things he went for and those are the things that I would like to think have always been part of Down football. The essence of Down teams is to go and win with style, go and play the game and don't try to be negative, don't try to stop the other team playing. That young team, that's the way they played.

'That team probably won too much, too soon. We were beaten by Cavan in 1969. I was captain of the side that day and I know that complacency was one of the major reasons that we were defeated. That's not to take away from a great Cavan display and they thoroughly deserved to win that game. But I feel that our preparations for that game were not what they should have been and we were an easier target for Cavan that day. That '69 Ulster final defeat for that young team was demoralising. The management team broke up then after that and while we won a number of Ulster championships in the 1970s, we never really made the impact at All-Ireland level that maybe we thought we should have made. That was a great disappointment to me personally because I knew there was a lot more in that squad.'

For his skill, contribution to football and exceptional performances, Seán O'Neill was voted Footballer of the Year in 1968. By then, he had won three All-Ireland senior medals with his county to add to the three National Football League medals secured in 1960, 1962 and 1968. The boost given by Down's success to football north of the border also ensured that he won eight Railway Cup medals with his province. Although his career was coming to a close at the time, he was also selected on the first two All-Star football teams in

1971 and 1972. A member of the Team of the Century and the Team of the Millennium, he was undoubtedly one of the finest forwards in the history of the game. Yet, somehow, despite all the accolades and awards, it is to Down's historic breakthrough in 1960 that the name of Seán O'Neill will always be linked.

'I think that it broke the ice,' Seán concludes. 'I think it was always going to be easier for Ulster teams and teams from the Six Counties to win after that. It certainly was always going to be easier for a Down team to go back and win again because there was that confidence there that if we had done it once we could do it again. To assess it in terms of Down football, it was breathtaking the impact it had inside the county. I have seen it in Donegal. I have seen it in Derry. These are firsts and the effect that it has not just in the sporting area but in the social area, in the feel-good factor among the people, is extraordinary.

'Suddenly, Down came of age. We were now a respected voice in the All-Ireland championship stakes. When a Down side went to Dublin we were expected to win. That is a major transformation. It's about attitude, it's about self-knowledge, it's about understanding what Down football is all about. We had great pride in the team and the achievement of the team. We had great pride in the players who achieved success and also great pride in the supporters who supported us. They were marvellous supporters; our supporters always were there to see us win and they never denigrated the side if we were beaten. I consider that I was very privileged to be a member of that team. It was a great, great privilege.'

4. ENDA COLLERAN

DARK TRAGEDY OVERSHADOWED GALWAY'S FIRST LEG OF THEIR HISTORIC THREE-IN-A- row in the 1960s. On 27 September 1964, as Galway captain John Donnellan held the Sam Maguire Cup aloft, little did he realise the misfortune that had befallen his family. Unbeknown to him, as he led Galway to their famous victory over Kerry his father had collapsed and died in the Hogan Stand. The death of Mick Donnellan, who was a former All-Ireland winner with Galway, cast a pall over proceedings as his body accompanied the Sam Maguire Cup on its long journey home. As a new generation of Donnellans joined the pantheon of All-Ireland winners, a star from another generation had passed to his eternal reward.

On that day in 1964 a second Galway legend died while watching the final. Sitting in his home in Galway, the great Mick Higgins, who captained his county to All-Ireland success in 1934, was overcome by the tension of the historic event. While watching the match on television he too passed away. It was a brace of events seared on the minds of all Galway's players, including their great right corner-back Enda Colleran. Soon to captain his county to two further successive All-Ireland titles, that extraordinary day when Galway won the first of their three-in-a-row was one he would never forget.

'I remember after half-time John Donnellan and I were walking out together to our respective positions,' Enda recalls. 'I was right full-back and he was right half-back and he turned to me and he said: "I think there's a row in the stand." In one portion of the stand there was an awful lot of people moving around and I said to him: "There must be." We didn't take any more notice at all. We played the second half and we won. We were in such good form but I noticed our officials were very subdued when they came in.

'We went into the dressing-room after all the presentations. John said: "I want to go out to show the cup to the old man." Up to that they couldn't get an opportunity to take him aside and tell him. At that stage they had to tell him and then everything changed. Actually, it wasn't a row at half-time but John's father had passed away in the stand. John's father had captained Galway and was a fantastic footballer. He died that day.

'It's amazing really, you think that an All-Ireland is the most important thing but everything changed, the atmosphere was totally subdued naturally enough and rightly so. The following evening the Sam Maguire Cup was brought home in the funeral cortège rather than triumphantly as it usually is. Amazingly, Mick Higgins, who played on the same Galway team as him, was actually watching the match at home and he collapsed and died as well. The rumour has it that Mick Donnellan went to heaven when he died and when he arrived at the gates St Peter said to him: "Who won the All-Ireland?" And he said: "Well, when I was leaving Galway were winning well but Mick Higgins will be up soon and he'll have the final score."'

Few players evoke fonder memories of Gaelic football in the 1960s than Enda Colleran from Moylough, County Galway. Captain of two of the Galway teams that won a famous three-in-a-row from 1964 to 1966, this accomplished defender and team leader was at the core of Galway's greatest years and deservedly won his place on the Team of the Century and the Team of the Millennium. He played at a time when Telefís Éireann was bringing visual images of Gaelic football into homes throughout the country for the very first time. Long before that, however, the young Enda Colleran was immersing himself in the rudiments of the game.

'I was lucky to be born in a lovely little village in north Galway called Moylough,' Enda says. 'My father was a farmer and we played football non-stop. I had three older brothers who had played for Galway at various stages. Anything I saw them try I usually tried it as well. We didn't have a football pitch in Moylough at the time. We played in the schoolyard each day with a small ball the size of a tennis ball and I think that helped us to practise our skills. At home in the evening it was non-stop, we played on the farm, we played at weekends and I was interested in nothing other than football. In national school I made out a scrapbook of Galway football even though at that stage you didn't have too many newspapers and no television. It shows how interested I was.

'I went to boarding-school at St Jarlath's College and I was really delighted with the football atmosphere there. Everybody talked, slept and ate football and I really enjoyed my time. We had a wonderful trainer who understood everybody's temperament. It was and still is a great feeder school for Galway football. If you were on a senior panel or a junior panel there, there was no way you could miss a training session. You had to be there unless you were sick in bed or whatever. There was a fantastic tradition of Gaelic football there.'

A wonderful prospect from the outset, Enda Colleran played on the famous Galway minor team that defeated Cork in the All-Ireland minor final of 1960. That team contained players like Noel Tierney, Séamus Leydon and Christy Tyrrell, who would later star on the Galway senior side in mid-decade. In the meantime, those young players lived in awe of Galway senior players like Mattie McDonagh, Frank Stockwell and Seán Purcell. It was one of those legends, Seán Purcell, who provided the inspiration for Enda to develop his football skills. The event occurred at the wedding of one of Enda's brothers who was a Galway senior footballer and who played with Purcell.

'Seán Purcell took me aside,' Enda remembers. 'He said to me: "I've watched you playing for Jarlath's and I've watched you playing for the Galway minors. I know you have the ability to make the Galway senior team if you knuckle down and train and practise your skills." Coming from Seán Purcell, who was the greatest footballer ever, I almost collapsed. I hung on his every word and took it in. I trained every single evening at home. There was a big hill and I would actually run up that hill until my legs couldn't carry me any more, then I would run down. I trained for the whole year.

'When it came to the trials for the Galway junior football team I was extremely fit and fitter than anybody else in the trials. I played two trials and I played very well. The team was picked to play Sligo in Tuam and I'll never forget it. I suppose it was very stubborn of me. I was a sub on the team and the renowned John Dunne, who trained all our All-Ireland winning teams, was calling to collect me on the Sunday morning to go to Tuam where the match was on. I remember my brother saying to me: "You're in Tuam today for the Sligo match." I said: "I'm not going." He said: "Why are you not going?" And I said: "Because I think I should be on the team."

'Not alone did I think I should be on the team but I firmly believed that I should if they were going to go by form in the trials. My brother said: "Oh, for God's sake, if you don't go today you'll never get the chance again to play for Galway." So John Dunne called at my house and he said to me: "OK, are you ready?" I said: " No, I'm sorry, I'm not going." He said: "Why are you not going?" I said: "Because I think I should be on the team." He called my brother and he said: "Will you come and talk a bit of sense into this young fellow?" I refused and I didn't travel. Galway won the match and the team was picked to play Mayo in the Connacht final and I was selected on that team. I was very lucky I wasn't ostracised from the Galway jersey for good at that stage.'

Enda Colleran soon progressed to the Galway senior team, where the foundations were already being laid for the future. In 1962, with Enda on the team, Galway were stymied by Roscommon in the Connacht final on a day when the crossbar broke with devastating consequences for the Tribesmen. In 1963 they edged past Kerry in the All-Ireland semi-final only to lose to Dublin in the championship decider by 1–9 to 0–10. Despite the lack of success it was clear that Galway football was back on track. The Tribesmen were emerging from the dip in fortunes that followed the county's 1956 All-Ireland success and the future looked rosy.

'In 1962 we played Roscommon in Castlebar in the Connacht final and that was the famous crossbar incident,' Enda says. 'A ball went over the bar and Aidan Brady, the Roscommon goalkeeper, swung off the crossbar and broke it. We were on top at that stage but there was a delay of about 12 minutes while the carpenters came and fixed the posts. Then Roscommon came back. Up to that Gerry O'Malley had done nothing. But Gerry had a new lease of life and he came forward time after time on his now well-renowned solo runs and brought the ball forward. Roscommon got two goals to beat us by a point. That was tragic but at the same time it showed promise.

'In '63 everything seemed to go well for us. We had a nice team with no stars to a certain extent. It was a very even team. I think the proof of that is that any of our players could play in nearly any position and most of them played at midfield for their clubs. We had a very good panel of footballers and we got on very well together. We had good teamwork and we looked good. In the All-Ireland final we had most of the play. Dublin got what I thought was a lucky goal and we were beaten narrowly. I remember after that game naturally enough we were heartbroken. But I remember in the dressing-room John Dunne saying to us: "You lost today and maybe you shouldn't have lost but I guarantee if you stay together you'll win next year." I think it was there and then we decided that next year was going to be our year.'

Galway's provincial campaign in 1964 took off with a win over Sligo and ended with victory over Mayo in the Connacht final. Having chalked up their second consecutive Connacht title, the Galway footballers moved on to the All-Ireland semi-final,where they accounted for Meath in a hard-fought battle. This was the second championship semi-final win in a row for this maturing Galway side. The evidence of how far they had come was to be witnessed in a tight match that concluded with the score-line of 1–8 to 0–9.

It was Kerry again in the championship decider, a team Galway had beaten in the previous year's semi-final. The Kerry side was captained by Niall Sheehy and packed with stars like Mick O'Dwyer, Mick O'Connell and Johnny Culloty. John Donnellan captained the Tribesmen. Unfortunately, the outcome was overshadowed by the deaths of John's father, Mick Donnellan, and of Galway legend Mick Higgins. Notwithstanding those tragedies, the Galway senior team had come of age to win the first of their famous three victories in a row by the convincing score of 0–15 to 0–10.

'After winning in '64 we had tremendous confidence, particularly after beating Kerry,' Enda says. 'Up to that, Galway didn't like playing Kerry and maybe had a complex about them. After that, those complexes were banished completely. We didn't fear the green and gold and we didn't fear the light blue of Dublin. We had wonderful confidence and that brought us through a lot of close encounters. When you have confidence like that, even if you are a few points down with let's say 15 minutes to go you say: "Look, if we get it together we're OK, we can win this game." That brought us through quite a few games that we won by a point or two.'

Inspired by the slogan 'Two All-Irelands back-to-back', Galway embarked on their championship campaign in 1965 with confidence and style. They had reason to be confident as they defeated Kerry in the 1965 National Football League final, reinforcing their dominance over the football kings from Munster. After winning their third consecutive Connacht title with victory over Sligo, they again progressed to the All-Ireland semi-final. In that penultimate match they beat Down with one of the finest performances of his career being provided by Enda Colleran.

Led by captain Enda Colleran, it was almost inevitable that Galway should face their now long-established rivals, Kerry, in the 1965 All-Ireland final. Enda marked J.J. Barrett. Kerry fielded many of the same stars of 1964, including Mick O'Connell, Mick O'Dwyer and Johnny Culloty. The men from the Kingdom were determined to avenge their previous defeats by Galway. However, the game concluded with a now familiar outcome, with Galway the winners by 0–12 to 0–9.

In 1966 Enda again captained the side but this time their All-Ireland final opponents were Meath. After securing their fourth Connacht title in a row, Galway narrowly beat Cork in the championship semi-final. They handily beat Meath by 1–10 to 0–7 in the All-Ireland final. Galway captain Enda Colleran had the rare distinction of lifting the Sam Maguire Cup for the second year in succession. It was Galway's first-ever three-in-a-row and the seventh All-Ireland in the county's football history.

'I was a little bit afraid of the role of captaincy with Galway,' Enda remarks. 'I was saying: "How am I going to react, am I going to be so nervous being captain that it's going to have an effect on my own game?" But I found that the responsibilities improved my game and in Jarlath's I had a little bit of experience with that because I was juvenile captain and I was captain of the Mountbellew team. In those days the captain didn't have much of a role except to toss the coin and lead the team out. But a captain always has a role behind the scenes. You have to be talking to all your players during the games and before the games and all that type of thing. If anything, it improved my own game.

'We had a lot of players who individually had great football skills and we had a lot of players who had the winning temperament. They were thoroughbreds in their own field and we had great camaraderie.

We looked forward to our training sessions and we enjoyed every one of them. We enjoyed the competition between us at the training sessions. I am led to believe that now players hate training sessions because they are nothing but run, run, run. We played soccer in our training sessions and we played Gaelic and we really concentrated on skills rather than running, running, running. I would admit that the players of today are much fitter than we were because they train as professional athletes. But in our time you had forwards who could kick the ball over the bar from 50 yards off their hand without much trouble. You don't have as many of them nowadays. They're fitter and faster but I think the skills have suffered a bit.'

Galway's victory in 1966 marked the end of an extraordinary run by the Tribesmen that established their place in Gaelic football history. The first team ever to achieve such a run was Dublin but that was back in the nineteenth century, from 1897 to 1899. Dublin repeated the achievement in the 1900s and in the 1920s. Of course, remarkable four-in-a-rows were accomplished by Wexford from 1915 to 1918 and twice by Kerry from 1929 to 1932 and from 1978 to 1981. Kerry also twice won three in succession. It was a remarkable triumph for Galway football to join such a select band of counties, adding another three-in-a-row to the history books and almost making it four in succession.

'The three-in-a-row was a wonderful achievement,' Enda agrees. 'TV was only emerging but even at that stage football meant everything to everybody, particularly in the countryside. I remember I wouldn't go to a dance before an All-Ireland semi-final because I was afraid it might interfere with my game. There were different attitudes and it was taken so seriously at the time. I can't see it being done again in the near future because first of all there's an awful lot of pressure on players. They all have high-powered jobs and they marry young or have young families. We were mostly teachers and it helped because we had the summer off. Also, I think now there are so many celebrations after winning an All-Ireland and the celebrations go on until Christmas at least and teams find it very difficult to come back for the following year. They may skip a year and come back and win another All-Ireland two years on.

'The Kerry team that almost won five-in-a-row in my opinion were the greatest team that I have ever seen. They were capable of winning five-in-a-row and they were unlucky that they didn't. They were a magnificent team. Until they came along we really thought ours was a fantastic achievement. Now we would agree that they were a much better team than we were. But to win three All-Irelands in a row and almost win a fourth, you had to have something. It's going to be a very difficult thing to achieve from now on.'

In 1968 Galway returned to the All-Ireland semi-final where they were defeated by Down. Two years later they were again semi-finalists, losing to Meath. In 1971 they lost the All-Ireland final to Offaly by the score of 1–14 to 2–8. The Tribesmen flirted with championship glory in the first half of the 1970s and were losing finalists in 1983. But, remarkably, it would take until 1998 for Galway to win another All-Ireland title. Few observers watching that great team of the mid-1960s would have predicted that 32 years would pass before the next All-Ireland championship triumph.

'My awful regret is that a lot of that team of the 1960s were kind of forced to retire or were dropped when they shouldn't have been,' Enda reflects. 'After '66 quite a few of the older players were kind of given the gentle hint to retire or were dropped. If that team got a rest and got back into intensive training, I have no doubt we could have won another one or two All-Irelands. I will believe forever that some players were dropped or forced to retire too soon. Maybe the selectors said: "After winning three this team is finished, we have to look for new players." Maybe that was the attitude but it was the wrong attitude.

'If you had said to me that Galway wouldn't win another All-Ireland until near the end of the century, I would have laughed. I would have laughed because I believed that Galway would be winning All-Irelands maybe once in every five years. Galway had quite good teams in the meantime but they didn't have the luck. You need luck as well as having good players to win an All-Ireland. They didn't have it. Things went against them in semi-finals and finals and then the pressure really comes on. If you go 20 or 25 years without winning, the pressure is really on for the guys who are playing.'

Throughout his career Enda Colleran became one of the finest right corner-backs in the history of the game. He combined the fielding and kicking skills of a great footballer with the organisational and inspirational skills of a fine captain. He added county championship medals to the many medals he acquired at college. He also added a Railway Cup medal won with Connacht in 1967 to the three senior All-Irelands, one National Football League and one minor All-Ireland he won with his county. A legend of the game for his exploits in the 1960s, he was a popular choice on both the Team of the Century and the Team of the Millennium.

'The 1960s was a great era,' Enda concludes. 'The 1960s music is still tops. You had Elvis coming along and you had all those kinds of things that keep reminding us of those great days. Whenever you hear 1960s music it brings you back again. We feel that we were young at the right time. I look back with great satisfaction and great pride. I really love to meet those guys again and every time we meet we relive all those occasions. We're very proud of our achievements.'

5. MICKEY KEARINS

STORIES OF MICKEY KEARINS' PROWESS IN SLIGO COLOURS ARE A DIME A DOZEN IN HIS native county. Old timers talk of 1971, when he scored 0–13 against Galway in the Connacht championship. Spectators boast of being there when he chalked up 0–14 against Mayo the following year. Fans describe the 0–13 he scored for Connacht in one match in 1972. In fact, for every year throughout the 1960s and up to his retirement in the late 1970s tales abound of how this extraordinary marksman single-handedly carried games to Sligo's opponents whether in championship contests, league campaigns or in friendly matches.

It is fair to say that Mickey Kearins was unfortunate in the county of his birth. Had he grown up in Galway he would most likely have shared in their three-in-a-row in the 1960s. Had he played for fellow Connacht counties Roscommon or Mayo, his cabinet would contain a healthier supply of provincial medals. Instead, he laboured with a poor, under-performing, ineffective Sligo senior side that by the time of his accession to senior status in 1961 had won just a single Connacht title – and that was back in 1928. No surprise then that the legendary Mickey Kearins became, like Clare's Jimmy Smyth in hurling, the greatest player never to win an All-Ireland football medal.

'Football in Sligo wasn't great at the time,' Mickey reflects. 'Sligo were at a low ebb. We never seemed to get a right good team at the one time. We were always short a couple of players. Even in the middle 1960s when we were going fairly well, we always seemed to be playing one or two backs in the forwards. We could always get maybe ten backs but we could get only one or two forwards. A back never makes a good forward.

'Sligo town would be strictly soccer and that wouldn't be much good to the Gaelic team, although we did have Gerry Mitchell and David Pugh, who both played with us for two or three seasons in the 1970s. We also never seemed to get too many inter-county players from north Sligo in those years. The county itself would be big enough but with north Sligo and Sligo town out of it, it left us with a smaller pick.

'I had finished in college in 1959 and there were trials for the minor team in '60. I was brought in and I happened to be selected at centre-field on the minor team in '60. I remember we were playing Mayo and a lot of the Mayo lads would have known me because it was in Mayo that I was in college. They couldn't understand how I had been picked at centre-field for the minor team and I couldn't even get on the college team. But I improved a fair bit over the year and I was also picked the next year on the minor team. Then I was picked on the senior team.

'At the time I arrived in Sligo football I really didn't know anybody on the county team. There was nobody from my own club on the team at that particular time. There was no collective training, which I was amazed at. You did your own training. It was only about 1962 or '63 that the collective training started and I thought that was a big improvement. We had an army man training us at the time and he stayed with us for three or four years. Sligo were improving a bit at the time. There was a terrible hunger among the players and I would say a greater hunger among the supporters. But always Galway seemed to be in the way; they always seemed to be the big team to beat. They were our bogey team.'

From the start of his senior career in 1961, it was clear that Mickey Kearins was a footballer of exceptional ability. Playing off both feet, he was almost literally a one-man band in Sligo's creaking attack. The great Seán Purcell describes days when Mickey took on Galway on his own. Other great players like Mick O'Connell testify to his wonderful ability. Not surprisingly he was Sligo's leading sharpshooter from the early 1960s to the mid-1970s. Whether it was picking off points from play or from frees, or scoring crucial goals for his county, few players could lay claim to the uncanny shooting skills of Mickey Kearins.

'When I started playing first I had a very weak left foot,' Mickey remarks. 'When I'd go out practising or training on my own I would continually keep kicking with my left foot to improve it. Eventually, it didn't matter to me which foot I was kicking with. I brought my left foot on to be just as good as my right. I practised shooting from play every day and I thought it was important to practise running with the ball. If you were in full-flight it was important that you could kick a point without slowing down, which a lot of players do. I felt I perfected that fairly well by practising. But I never practised the frees; I felt the more I practised them the worse I would get at them so I left it for the day of the game.

'My role on the team was mostly to try and get as many scores as I could. Every time the backs would get the ball they'd look to see where I was positioned and they'd try to get the ball to me. It wasn't always that easy. Some of our forwards maybe weren't up to the mark and if the opposing team took me out of the game they had most of the scoring power taken away from Sligo. When there were two or three marking you it was always a difficulty to get scores. But there were days when the ball might play better for you and no matter who was playing on you, they wouldn't be able to mark you. If I didn't score three or four points from play in a game I felt I didn't play well. Taking the frees was my job. But if any forward isn't getting three or four points from play in a game, he's definitely not worth his place on the team.'

The three-in-a-row All-Ireland winning Galway senior football team provided the measure for any football player or team in Connacht in the 1960s. In that decade, Galway powered their way through the province, winning six of the nine Connacht finals they contested. In sharp contrast, Sligo's status in the province was reflected in their single appearance in the 1965 Connacht final, where they narrowly lost to Galway by 1–12 to 2–6. Few teams could survive Galway's glorious days in the sun. Mayo and Leitrim suffered from Galway's success. After a promising start to the decade, Roscommon also dropped off the pace. If you weren't from Galway, the 1960s were frustrating years in Connacht football.

'Our matches with Galway always were close,' Mickey recalls. 'In those years they never gave us a big beating but they always seemed to manage to get those two or three points to beat us. In 1965 we had a reasonably good team. Galway beat us by three points in the

Connacht final and they went on to win the All-Ireland. We had played them in '64 and they beat us in that Connacht championship as well. After beating us then, they also went on to win the All-Ireland. So we were there or thereabouts on a number of occasions but never made the breakthrough.

'I would have rated all those Galway lads highly. The three-in-a-row team were one of the best teams. Kerry and the Down team of 1960 and 1961 I would probably have rated as better but Galway were a very fit team and had some great players as well. They always seemed to have the upper hand on us. I honestly think they had better players than us. We probably had nine or ten very good players but we were always short two or three to make it a very good team. I would also say Galway believed in themselves much more than we did.

'I played Railway Cup football with them and they were a great bunch of lads. I knew them very well because I played Railway Cup with them for six or seven years on the trot. Noel Tierney was probably one of the great full-backs of our time. Martin Newell and John Donnellan and Bosco McDermott were great backs. Then they had great forwards in Séamus Leydon, Cyril Dunne, Christy Tyrrell and Mattie McDonagh. The comradeship between them was so good that I'd say that's why they were so successful as a team.

'In '65 we played them in the Gael Linn Cup final and we happened to beat them even though they were All-Ireland champions at that time. We got a trip to Wembley out of it. But I would say most people in England didn't want to see Sligo coming to Wembley, they were hoping it would be Galway that would win the tournament. It was the only time I think we beat Galway in those years.'

The Galway–Sligo rivalry was renewed right from the start of the 1970s, with Galway running out narrow winners in the 1970 provincial semi-final. Things were improving for Sligo at the time. In 1968 their minor footballers had won a provincial title for the first time since 1949. They progressed to the All-Ireland minor final, where Cork beat them by the tight score-line of 3–5 to 1–10. Many of Sligo's young players soon filtered through to the senior team, where they togged out alongside veterans like Mickey Kearins. With Mickey playing some of the finest football of his career, the stage was set for one of Sligo's greatest football eras. A thrilling 1971 Connacht final saw Sligo lose in a replay to Galway. In 1973 the teams fought another tense provincial battle, with Galway again emerging as narrow winners. It seemed that Sligo might achieve success after all.

'In 1970 and '71 and '72 I was playing probably better than ever and the county were going well at that time as well,' Mickey reflects. 'We had a good minor team in '68. They went to the All-Ireland where Cork beat them by a point. Five or six of that team came into the senior team in 1970. That's why the 1970, '71, '72 team was better than anything I had played with in the 1960s. That team I thought were unlucky not to make the breakthrough. If we did get that bit of luck that time, in '70 or '71, we might have achieved something.

'In the early '70s we happened to meet Galway again. There were a lot of changes on the Galway team from the 1960s. Most of the three-in-a-row team were gone. Jimmy Duggan and Liam Sammon were probably the only ones that had survived. We met them in the Connacht final in Castlebar in 1971 and it was a draw. I got 13 points against them. There were eight of them from frees and five from play, which I think was a fairly good return. Five points from play for any forward is fairly good.

'We had to go back to Castlebar for the replay and they beat us by a point after another epic encounter. There was a funny incident in the first of those games. We got a sideline ball with minutes to go and we were a point down. The crowd were pushing in on the sideline. As I was running up to take the sideline kick, Tull Dunne, who was the manager of the Galway team, caught me by the leg and I fell before I got to the ball. The referee brought the ball in about five yards from the sideline, which gave me a better chance. I kicked it over the bar for the equaliser. Mr Dunne catching me by the leg gave me the five yards I needed to get the score.'

The pinnacle of Sligo's football years was scaled in 1975, when the county not only won their first Connacht title since 1928 but also reached the dizzy heights of an All-Ireland semi-final. There was hysteria in Sligo. On the road to Croke Park, Sligo had defeated Galway in the Connacht championship for the first time in 28 years. Mayo had been cast aside in the provincial final, after which Mickey Kearins had been carried shoulder-high from the pitch. The only problem was that Kerry were the opponents in the All-Ireland semi-final. Little did anyone realise at the time that the very same Kerry team would soon embark on one of the finest runs in football history. Sligo were about to enter the lion's den. The final score told its own story: Kerry 3–13, Sligo 0–5.

'It was a big breakthrough for Sligo,' Mickey says of the county's historic Connacht victory. 'We played the Connacht final in Sligo and it was a draw. Everybody felt that we had lost our chance. Sligo going to Castlebar was never that successful for us. But the team played really well in Castlebar in the replay. There was only a point in it at the end. The supporters and the players really went wild afterwards because we were the underdogs, especially after going to Castlebar. The minute the game was over the Sligo supporters were all over us. I can't remember much about the homecoming but I know we were playing Kerry two or three weeks afterwards.

'For a start we weren't near as fit as Kerry were. They were faster to the ball, they were sharper and I would also say that at the time they were a way better team than any other team in Ireland. I think they even surprised themselves, they were so dominant for a number of years. We were holding them reasonably well until Sligo moved John Brennan out the field from full-back. That opened the floodgates fully for them. They got three goals fairly quickly after that. But they were going to beat us anyhow because they were so superior. My impression was that Kerry were just far too good for us.

'Then they met Dublin in the final and they annihilated Dublin as well. I thought that this young Kerry team would go on and win ten-in-a-row, but Dublin with a great manager in Kevin Heffernan had them well sized up and took them in 1976 and '77. Kerry proved to be a great team. They came back and won it then four years on the trot, missed two years and won it three on the trot. I honestly wouldn't think there was any team I saw that could compare with that great Kerry team. It was an outstanding team all over.'

Sligo's great run in 1975 came too late in the day to save football in the county. The mainstay of the team, Mickey Kearins, was ageing fast and his days in the black and white shirt were numbered. Other players faced retirement and duly hung up their boots. As Mickey says: 'The team were just going over the hill a bit. I felt the team were too old.' In addition, instead of boosting confidence the semi-final against Kerry seemed to reinforce old beliefs that Sligo footballers could never succeed. Rather than prompting a football revival, the entire opposite happened. Sligo slumped back into the doldrums.

For Mickey Kearins, the dream of marching out at Croke Park in an All-Ireland final was all but gone. He had, however, experienced the magic of Croke Park in a different context, representing his province in Railway Cup matches. For an extraordinary 13 successive seasons he was selected for Connacht, where he played alongside the finest footballers from neighbouring counties. Those campaigns resulted in two Railway Cup medals, which were won in 1967 and 1969.

'It was a great occasion for a player like myself from one of the weaker counties,' Mickey says. 'I got to play with the likes of the great Galway lads and I got to play against the great men from Kerry and Down. The likes of Packie McGarty and Gerry O'Malley and myself may not have got to Croke Park only for Railway Cup games. It was a great chance for us to meet the rest of the players as well. We wouldn't have had the chance of meeting them only for the Railway Cup games.

'In '67 we were playing Ulster on a terrible breezy day in Croke Park. We had the breeze in the first half but we weren't doing too well. I think we were leading by two or three points. I got a goal about two minutes from half-time. We were playing against a gale force breeze in the second half and I don't think we got many scores but we held on to win by a point. I think that Ulster team were going for five medals on the trot. We were lucky to hold on that day and it was my first medal in any competition.

'In '69 we beat Munster and I think we beat them well. I only played in the first half. I came off injured early on in the game, after maybe 20 minutes. I had a suspect ankle going into the game and I didn't last too long. Connacht won easily that day. That time in Croke Park I think there were over 20,000 people for the games. It was a great loss to the weaker counties when the Railway Cup died away. Towards the end, there wouldn't be 700 at them. It was a wonderful competition for us.'

When the first All-Star selection was made in 1971, it was no surprise that Mickey Kearins was chosen for one of the prestigious awards. The only disappointment is that it was the only All-Star he'd ever receive. The truth is that there were no medals or awards sufficient to compensate Mickey Kearins for his contribution to Sligo football. Whether it was playing for his county or winning innumerable league and championship titles with his club, St Patrick's, no other player even approached the mark he made.

Along with his playing role, he simultaneously managed Sligo for a number of years. Following his retirement he became a top-class referee. He also, of course, won that famous Connacht senior championship medal in 1975 to add to the two Railway Cup medals won in 1967 and 1969. But it was for his marvellous solo runs and side-swerves, his effortless style and deadly accuracy from play or from frees that Mickey will always be remembered. Having scored some 36 goals and 1,158 points for his county, no other player dominated Sligo football quite like the great Mickey Kearins.

'I retired in '78 because I had lost interest,' Mickey says. 'In 1971 Galway beat us in a replayed Connacht final and in 1972 Mayo beat us in another replay. After that I think my game started to slip a bit and I'd say my best years were over after '72. We went to America with our club team in '74 and I never bothered to train much after I came back. I felt that after 12 or 13 years I had given it a lot. I always did enjoy going to training but after '74 I wasn't enjoying any evening at training. Eventually, I decided to call it a day.

'I was disappointed that I didn't have an All-Ireland medal. That's probably the biggest occasion. Even to play on All-Ireland final day would be a wonderful achievement and you would be disappointed not to be there. Even when you go to the All-Ireland final as a spectator and you see the players coming out and preparing for the throw-in, it surely is a wonderful occasion. I felt it would be wonderful to be there on that day. I regret that I didn't get the chance to play on All-Ireland final day but there's not much we can do about it.

'It's very important to have new winners of the All-Ireland series. It's wonderful for football when that happens. If you go back and look at Donegal in '92 that was their first time ever to win the All-Ireland. You had all the schools involved and children wearing the jerseys with the players' names on their backs. It would be great for football in Sligo if something like that happened. The most important thing in a county when they win an All-Ireland is that every young boy in school has a ball or a hurley with him, depending on what code is followed. The schools would have the boys with the jerseys and the names up on the back of them. That's why the schools in Kerry are so good, the same in Galway. Hopefully, it will happen with Sligo in the near future.

'I've really enjoyed it. If you said to me: "What have you won for the 18 years you were playing?" I couldn't show you very much in the line of medals. But Gaelic football has been fairly good to me in my job travelling all over Ireland. I would hardly need an introduction in any county, everybody knows me from Gaelic games. I have no regrets, we had some great days and I'm glad that I played and met so many great players. I enjoyed it immensely and I met some wonderful people through the game, which I never would if I wasn't playing inter-county football. I dream that some day Sligo might surprise everybody and get to an All-Ireland final. I had plenty of dreams when I was playing myself but none of them ever came true. It's the same old story with Sligo. I felt we were always short a few players to make the big breakthrough. But that's life and that's Sligo football.'

6. BILLY MORGAN

IT WAS HARDLY SURPRISING THAT THE CORK FOOTBALL TEAM TURNED TO RELIGION IN the lead-up to the 1973 All-Ireland final. With 28 barren years behind them, invoking God's powers seemed exactly what was needed. Clearly, the traditional pre-match mass or the occasional player making the sign of the cross would not suffice. Accompanying those rituals were individual personal blessings for players and the carrying of a recently deceased, former player's sacred scapulars onto the pitch.

Whether or not God heard Cork's call is unknown. In truth, he was probably equally impressed by the fervour of Galway. But that day in September 1973 there was no doubting the power of the scapulars previously worn by former Cork legend Weeshie Murphy which were pinned to the shirt of Cork captain Billy Morgan. Nor could Cork's opponents match the personal blessings bestowed on the Rebels by a brother of one of the players, Kevin Jer O'Sullivan. For the record, the team's supplications resulted in Cork's fourth All-Ireland title, with a 3–17 to 2–13 victory over Galway.

'I remember the blessing well,' Cork's goalie and captain, Billy Morgan, recalls. 'We were staying in the Skylon Hotel in Drumcondra and the morning of the match we were down kicking around in St Patrick's College. Kevin Jer had a brother who was a priest and he came to give us his blessing. We were all kneeling down and he was going around to each one of us. When he came around to Donal Hunt, who was known not to be terribly religious, Hunt looked up at him with a look as if to say: "What's this mumbo-jumbo about?" Of course, when we all saw him blessing Hunt and Hunt looking at him with a "What's this about?" look, we all just burst out laughing. It lightened the whole scene. It released the pressure a bit.

'Con Murphy came to the hotel on the morning of the match. He wasn't a doctor at the time; he was a student and a friend of mine. I knew his mother well and I was quite friendly with his father Weeshie. Con's mother asked me would I wear the scapulars that Weeshie wore in the '45 All-Ireland. I pinned them onto the inside of my jersey and I wore them during the game.

'There's quite a funny story about those same scapulars because in 1987, when we played Meath, Conor Counihan was captain and Con Murphy told me that he asked Conor to wear them. Conor did the same as I did; he pinned them to the inside of the jersey that he wore. But when the game was over and Meath had beaten us, he swapped his jersey with some Meath player. When he came into the Cork dressing-room, Con asked for his scapulars. "Oh, Jesus," Conor said and he ran out of the Cork dressing-room into the Meath dressing-room looking for his jersey. The Meath fellows thought he wanted his jersey back but he was only looking for the scapulars. He found them anyway and brought them back.

'How serious players were about their religion I don't know but in Dublin, on the morning of a match, we always had mass said in the hotel and everybody would go. I'd be a practising Catholic and always have been. I'd always make sure I'd go to mass and communion. Most would receive, too. It's possibly superstitious in a way that we didn't want the man above against us before we went out.'

Few Cork players contributed more to the game of football than the county's inspirational goalkeeper, All-Ireland winning captain and enormously successful coach, Billy Morgan. An All-Ireland winner as Cork captain in 1973, he eventually coached his county to two further All-Ireland successes in 1989 and 1990. Known for his leadership and organisational skills and also for his ability to motivate and draw the best from players, not surprisingly he was associated with three of the Rebel County's greatest years. Before Billy's era, the county's only other successes were in 1890, 1911 and 1945.

Ironically, Billy's football career started out not in goals but as a forward with the Cork minor football team. A talented outfield player, he soon turned to soccer with Tramore Athletic, where he first played in nets. 'Being a Gaelic player they put me in goal,' Billy explains. 'The following year, when I was in UCC, they were looking for a goalkeeper and I was put in goal with UCC. I never intended staying there but I got on the Cork U-21s and then the Cork seniors so I stayed in goal then.

'At that time I used to see Gaelic football goalkeepers and anything high that came in around the square they'd punch it away. First of all I always tried to catch it and the second thing was I tried to use the ball sensibly, not just boot it back out the field. I'd give it to a corner-back or to a half-back. A lot of people say that's what I brought to the game. I felt it was stupid just kicking the ball back out the field when it came back in to you just as fast. My idea was to try and keep it and keep possession.'

Having arrived on the Cork U-21 scene, Billy Morgan participated in the county's unsuccessful All-Ireland U-21 final battle with Kildare in 1965. After a solid performance in that championship encounter he was elevated to the Cork senior panel. Following a successful début in a challenge game against Offaly, Billy became a regular in the Cork nets. The Rebels won the Munster championship in 1966, eventually getting knocked out in the All-Ireland semi-final by Galway. In 1967 they won Munster again after beating Kerry for the second year in a row. This time they made it to the ultimate stage of the championship with a date against Meath in September. Unfortunately, Cork lost by 1–9 to 0–9, with a tragic goal deciding the outcome.

'Meath got this goal which was a disaster in a way,' Billy recalls. 'They got a 14-yard free straight in front of the goal. Tony Brennan took it and he failed to rise it. It went straight into the hands, I think, of Jerry Lucey, who belted the ball back out to the middle of the field. When Tony Brennan took the free we lined the goal, naturally enough, and when Jerry cleared it everybody ran back out the field with the exception of Meath's Terry Kearns. He stayed by the goalposts, leaning on his knees, taking a breather.

'Matt Kerrigan of Meath caught the ball in the middle of the field and he lobbed it back in. I knew Terry Kearns was there and my initial thing was to punch it away. Denis Coughlan was coming back and my first intention was to knock it away to Denis but I changed my mind. I tried to catch it. I thought I was well clear of Terry Kearns but I jumped and he was underneath me, he put up his fist, it just caught the back of his fist and went over my shoulder and into the back of the net.

'I still remember it like it was yesterday. It was a goal that should never have happened. Looking back on it I think he was extremely lucky because he just stuck up his fist and it could have gone anywhere. It could have gone over the bar or it could have gone wide. I should have stuck to my first thing, to knock it away. Even if the ball had gone over the bar from Tony Brennan's free, which 99 times out of 100 it would have, we might have won. But it does rankle when I think that if I stuck to my original intentions of knocking the ball away we might have won.'

It took until 1973 for the Cork senior footballers to return to an All-Ireland final and by then the team was transformed. In came players fresh from Cork's victorious march to a series of All-Ireland minor and All-Ireland U-21 championships in the early 1970s. New names like Jimmy Barry-Murphy and Ray Cummins appeared on Cork team-sheets. The new blood brought renewed vigour and style to the senior panel. It wasn't until 1973, however, that the team returned to Croke Park for the September decider. Having beaten Kerry in Munster and having destroyed Tyrone in the semi-final, Cork then beat Galway in the championship final by 3–17 to 2–13.

'It was hugely important,' Billy says of that 1973 victory. 'It was 28 years since Cork last won a senior football All-Ireland and the longer it was going on the harder it was becoming. When we came out I kicked the ball up in the air. It went away over into the middle of the field. We were called to sit down for our photograph straight away. The ball was lying there in the middle of the field and while we were having the photograph taken the Galway team came out. They came down to the Hill 16 end and they took the ball, they just picked it up and kicked away with it among their own.

'When our photograph was taken, I went down to get the ball back off Liam Sammon. I said: "You've a ball belonging to us there." He didn't argue the point but I thought he looked nervous and he was breathless and he just gave me a ball straight away. Then we had to line up in front of the stand and I thought they looked very nervous or seemed edgy. I just remember saying it to our players at the time, going down the line and saying: "They're nervous, let's take it to them right from the start."

'When the ball was thrown in they got a free from about 50 yards out and they put the ball over the bar. From the kick-out we went straight up the field and got a goal. Jimmy Barry-Murphy palmed it into the net. That put us in front and put them on the back foot straight away. That was inside a few minutes and for the rest of that half we took the game to them. In that first half we were going at them in waves and we were well ahead at half-time.

'To give them their due they made a fight-back in the second half and brought it down to three points. They got a goal and I remember it well. At the time I didn't think the ball had crossed the line but photographs afterwards showed it did. Tommy Naughton, I think, took a shot and I dived and pushed it up against the post. I fell up against the post and it fell back over me. When I turned around it wasn't over the line and I picked it up and went out. But the umpire was waving the green flag. At the time I said the ball wasn't over the line but a photograph in the paper the following day showed that it had crossed the line.

'That brought them back to three points and they looked to be on a roll. But again we reasserted ourselves and kept them at bay. Then Jimmy Barry-Murphy got a goal with seven minutes to go. It was the greatest feeling of euphoria that I ever had because I said: "It's all over now." I think there was a photograph of me on my knees when that goal went in. Even though they got another goal in injury time, we went down and got a third.

'From the minute the full-time whistle went all the Cork people came on the pitch. I remember being up in the stand and looking down and there was a sea of red and white out in front. At that stage the dressing-rooms were under the Cusack Stand so we had to get across from the Hogan. I remember being carried across and being pulled all over the place with the enthusiasm. Then we went back to the Skylon and I think there was a champagne reception for us and again there were huge crowds. That night we had a banquet out in the Green Isle.

'What I will never forget was the homecoming. When we got into Cork there were crowds in the station and all the way up MacCurtain Street. The biggest thing is when we turned Barry's corner; looking down onto Patrick Street it was just a sea of people. I never saw anything like it before. You couldn't see the bridge, you couldn't see the streets; it was just people all the way down to the Savoy.

'People have told me about the homecoming after the '66 All-Ireland hurling final. Fellows like Charlie McCarthy and Gerald McCarthy told me about it. But until you see it or experience it you can't really describe it. I know in 1989, when the footballers were coming back, Teddy McCarthy who had experienced it coming back in '86 with the Cork hurlers said the lads won't believe this until they turn Barry's corner. He was dead right, it was something else just to see all those people. You think: "How the hell is the bus going to get through all these?" But there was nobody killed.

'That '73 team was an excellent team and my regret was that we didn't win more, that we only won that one All-Ireland. We celebrated long and with Cork being a big county everyone wanted the cup and everyone wanted it to travel down through their town or village. We were only too willing to do it. I remember Donie O'Donovan, who was a very shrewd man, warning us after Christmas that now the celebrations should stop and we should get down to winning another All-Ireland. But we didn't really heed his words.

'I remember we went to San Francisco that spring and he warned us again. He gave us a stern warning this time that if we wanted to keep celebrating we may as well forget about an All-Ireland. We were all nice and polite to Donie but the celebrations didn't stop and it cost us, I would think. It was an awful pity because definitely there was more than one All-Ireland in us.'

As so often happens in Cork football history, neighbours Kerry were the rock the team foundered upon in the years ahead. Cork did beat Kerry in the 1974 Munster final but fell by the wayside against Dublin in the All-Ireland semi-final. Looking at both those matches, observers would have been hard-pressed to spot the huge revivals that were about to take place in the Kerry and Dublin camps. Ominously for Cork, the explosive lift-off of Kevin Heffernan's Dublin and Mick O'Dwyer's Kerry was only just about to take place. In the new competitive environment, the Rebels would lose the next eight Munster finals in succession to a great Kerry team. It goes without saying that visits to Croke Park were out of the question.

'First of all, Kevin Heffernan raised the bar where fitness levels were concerned,' Billy reflects. 'Then Mick O'Dwyer took over in Kerry and he followed in Dublin's footsteps and concentrated first and foremost on getting a very fit team. They were a young Kerry team and they surprised us in 1975 in Killarney. They were much fitter than us and beat us fairly comprehensively.

'The real turning point was '76, when we regrouped. We drew the Munster final and had them beaten in the replay except for two controversial decisions where a goal was given to Kerry and we had one disallowed. I wonder if Cork won that game, which we should have, what would have happened to Kerry afterwards? Having said that, Kerry went rolling on. From the team that won the All-Ireland in '75 they gained a few very important players. Eoin Liston was one, the last piece in the jigsaw, but also Jack O'Shea and Seán Walsh came in and they became very, very strong.

'I know Mick O'Dwyer used to come into the dressing-room after every Munster final and he'd try to console us by saying: "Look, if it's any consolation you're the second-best team in Ireland." To be quite honest, it cut very little ice with me because I was so dejected. Every year we used to train like dogs and always felt we had a chance. We never left anything to chance yet we always came up short because they were so good.

'Talking to some of their players years later they always said they prepared for the Cork game like it was an All-Ireland final. They took no chances against us. They were better than us and it showed. I think it was eight years they beat us on the trot and it was frustrating year in year out to put in such a huge effort and to walk off the pitch well-beaten by Kerry.'

Billy Morgan played in the Munster final in 1981, where he was carried off following an accidental clash with Eoin Liston. He ended his Cork career shortly afterwards, following which he departed for America where he studied for a postgraduate degree in physical education. He returned, however, as coach to the Cork team where he applied the vast know-how he had accumulated both academically and on the field of play.

From 1987 to 1990, as coach, he inspired Cork to four All-Ireland finals in a row, winning two. It began with All-Ireland defeats against Meath in 1987 and 1988. The first of those finals Meath won convincingly by 1–14 to 0–11. The second, however, was a rancorous affair, bringing victory to Meath in a replay by the narrowest of margins, 0–13 to 0–12.

'Meath and Cork came to the fore around the same time,' Billy recalls. 'In the 1987 final we looked like winning at the start. We were four or five points up at one stage and we missed a goal. Then they got a goal and I'd say their experience in 1986, when they were in the semi-final against Kerry, stood to them. They beat us well in the second half and we had no complaints.

'In 1988 we felt that we were ready, that we had a year's experience behind us. I thought we played them off the pitch. We drew the game when we should have won it. In the drawn game Dinny Allen had caught Mick Lyons with his elbow, Barry Coffey had tackled Colm O'Rourke and caught him with his shoulder behind the ear. I saw those two. They say Niall Cahalane is supposed to have caught Brian Stafford. I didn't see that one. But all the talk between the drawn game and the replay was that Meath were going to sort us out. My own instructions were that if that was the case, if there was any trouble stand together and be united.

'As it happened, Gerry McEntee hit Niall Cahalane, there was a bit of a flare-up and all of our fellows got involved. When it was over and McEntee was sent off, I said to our fellows: "OK now, that's it, we'll play football from here on in, no retaliation." I repeated it at half-time. It was the biggest mistake I ever made as a manager. I think I should have said: "Meet fire with fire and if necessary we'll finish this game ten-a-side." We should have won it as it was, with Meath down to 14 men for most of the game. But fair play to Meath, they won it with the 14 men. You shouldn't lose those games but we did.'

In the next two years Cork made up for the disappointments of 1987 and 1988 by powering their way to two historic senior All-Irelands in a row. For a county with only four prior All-Irelands to their credit and with the first of those dating back to 1890, the achievement was nothing short of remarkable. Adding to Cork's joy were the Munster final victories over Kerry, which the Rebels extended to a substantial four-in-a-row in 1990. The first of the All-Ireland finals involved victory over Mayo by 0–17 to 1–11, a narrower margin than experts predicted. The second of the victories was over old adversaries Meath by 0–11 to 0–9.

'Nothing will ever take away from or surpass winning an All-Ireland as a player,' Billy reflects. 'I always say that managing or coaching is second to playing. You can't beat playing and that 1973 All-Ireland senior medal will surpass anything I've won as a manager. But having said all that, 1989 and 1990 gave me immense satisfaction. They were great years.

'I'd like to think we should also have won in '88, it was one that definitely got away from us. It was coming to a period where it was very difficult to win two-in-a-row never mind three-in-a-row because of the intensity of preparation. I don't want to take from Meath or bring up any old sores but I felt we should have won the '88 final. I have no ill-feeling or any regrets or any malice towards Meath. In fact, I often use the Meath will-to-win in dressing-rooms. If only Cork teams had their burning desire to win!'

Despite a bitter run-in with the Cork County Board over the matter of nominating selectors, Billy Morgan stayed on as coach of the Cork senior footballers until 1996. Although Cork achieved further success in Munster and reached the championship decider against Derry in 1993, the county failed to win any more All-Irelands. Billy had by then, however, established his name as one of the great Cork legends, remembered not alone for coaching his county to a remarkable two-in-a-row but also for captaining his county to a famous All-Ireland victory back in 1973.

'For years Cork football was my life and I dedicated everything to it,' Billy concludes. 'I would like to think that it was a very successful period for Cork football. They were a great bunch of lads. I'm sure you've heard that before but they were. I'm great friends with all of them. I love meeting them. We meet every Christmas when a gang of us goes out for a drink. They were great years and I enjoyed every minute of them. I have no regrets and I look back on the years with great pleasure.'

7. JIMMY KEAVENEY

ONE EVENING IN MAY 1974 AN UNLIKELY PHONE CALL WAS MADE TO AN EQUALLY unlikely footballer to spearhead what was planned to be the fittest team in Gaelic football. The call was made by Dublin manager Kevin Heffernan to a retired inter-county player by the name of Jimmy Keaveney. Heffernan's plan was simple: to create the fittest team in Ireland, whose stamina and skills would outlast the best that other teams could offer. The only problem was that Jimmy Keaveney was in his late 20s, unfit, overweight and was out of inter-county football for two years.

As football history shows, that phone call in the late spring of 1974 could not have been more inspired. Although aged 29, the return of Keaveney helped propel Dublin to heights never seen before. A lethal sharpshooter, he helped his county to six consecutive All-Ireland finals, winning three. Along the way he twice became Footballer of the Year, won three All-Star awards and scored a record 2–6 in the 1977 All-Ireland final.

'I had started playing with Dublin in 1964,' Jimmy recalls. 'I was 19 years of age and we won a Leinster championship in '65. I came in on the tail-end of a good Dublin team that won the '63 All-Ireland final. We then went through a rough period. In '67 we got to a league final and we were beaten. After that nothing happened at all. I decided in '72, after Kildare beat us in the Leinster championship, that I'd had my fill of it. The training wasn't properly organised, you had half the team out training and I was having more *craic* and enjoying my football more with my club, St Vincent's. I decided to finish in '72.

'In May 1974 Dublin were playing Wexford in the first round of the Leinster championship in Croke Park. I watched the game up on

Hill 16 and I left the match and went off with a few lads probably down to Meagher's pub, had a few pints and went home. Then on the Monday night I was in the house and I got a phone call from Kevin Heffernan. Kevin says: "Jimmy, is there any chance you'd change your mind and come back down and do a bit of training? I want to get you back in the team and get you in some kind of shape for the coming championship." I had known Kevin all my life and I played with him as well and I knew how persuasive he was. There was no sense in arguing because if he wanted me back he was going to get me back one way or the other.

'I ended up going down on the Tuesday night to Parnell Park to train. I remember after about 40 minutes my head just went light and I remember Stephen Rooney helping me over to the sideline for me to sit down. I just wasn't used to it and I never saw anything like the level of training that Heffernan was doing. It all started there. After that I just had to get fit and the roller-coaster started taking off.

'Everything in life was secondary, your family, your job, everything was secondary to that Dublin team. We trained on a Tuesday and a Thursday. It was very tough training. We were there for an hour and a half to two hours training hard. At no stage would you be standing, you'd be moving all the time. Then Kevin decided to bring in this Saturday training. I thought: "Is the man gone off his head or something?" We were training on a Saturday with a match on a Sunday.

'The funny thing about it was that before I came back I used to go to St Vincent's club on a Friday night for a game of cards and a couple of pints. When I went back training with Dublin and he introduced the Saturday morning training, I was still nipping down to Vincent's. The second time I was down there, who arrives in only Heffernan! He says: "Obviously, Jimmy, you're not taking this training seriously." I said: "Why, what's wrong?" He said: "We're training tomorrow morning and here you are drinking pints. God only knows what time you'll go home at!"

'Eventually I said to myself: "Obviously, he's taking it seriously." So I stopped it. But it still didn't stop him from going down the following two Friday nights to see if I was there. The lads would tell him: "He's down in Meagher's." And he drove down to Meagher's looking for me. I was at home in the house. That's how seriously it was taken and I realised that if Kevin and the rest of the lads were putting this effort into the team, there's no sense in me messing them about. I said I'd either get out or stay with them. I stayed with them and I did as much training as the rest of the lads.'

Dublin's revival in the 1970s effectively began with victory over Cork in the All-Ireland semi-final in 1974. The Rebels entered the match as reigning All-Ireland champions and had just defeated Kerry in the Munster final. With players like Jimmy Barry-Murphy, Cork were clear favourites to progress to the 1974 championship decider. However, despite a Barry-Murphy goal it was Dublin that pulled off a shock victory. In September, with the help of some vital points from Jimmy Keaveney, they compounded their progress with victory over Galway in the championship decider. The Dublin machine had sprung into action.

'I remember coming up to the Cork game, ' Jimmy says. 'We did the usual bit of training on Saturday and normally we would have a team-talk amongst the players. But Kevin Heffernan decided not to have it. He said: "I want to address you lads." I remember it was in the old shed in Parnell Park. If we could have got at Cork when that meeting was over we would have destroyed them. He built us up so much that I went home saying: "Shag this, we're not going to lose tomorrow." Prior to that I was happy enough to come out of Leinster.

'It's a coincidence that Billy Morgan, who is a very good friend of mine, and Frank Cogan are married to twin sisters and the two girls were actually staying in my house on the Saturday night. Cork had dropped Frank Cogan much to everybody's surprise. I thought Frank was a great corner-back and I remember Kevin Heffernan talking about him. He was delighted to see Frank Cogan not playing. So we were in the house that night and we got up and got mass the following morning. Ann Cogan said to me: "Jimmy, can I ring Cork to see did Frank travel up for the game?" There was no answer and Mary Morgan said to Ann: "Ah sure, he might be playing in the final." I said: "Hold on a second, girls. You haven't won the semi-final yet!"

'The lovely thing about it was that when we beat Cork the first two people I met after the match outside the dressing-room waiting on me were Mary Morgan and Ann Cogan. It was a lovely touch. That started it off. Once we got over Cork we were quite convinced we'd beat Galway because Galway had already lost two All-Ireland finals in the previous three years. Fresh after the Cork game nobody was going to stand in our way. We went into the game and we felt that after beating Cork this could be our one and only chance not alone to play in an All-Ireland final but to win it.

'The Galway game was the highlight of my career. There were fellows like Cullen, O'Driscoll, Doherty, Hanahoe and myself, who had been there for up to ten years and done nothing. We were all hitting 28 or 29 years of age at the time and we thought we'd never win an All-Ireland. I thought we were an average team. We were after getting the breaks that year and we were so determined to beat Galway. There was no way we were going to get beaten. I know Paddy Cullen saved a penalty but I still feel that if the penalty went in we were strong enough and good enough to come back and beat them. I felt totally confident that day.'

It was no surprise that 72,000 spectators turned up for the 1974 All-Ireland final. Nor was it surprising that the majority travelled to Croke Park in various shades of blue. They came from all walks of life, straddling different social classes and various sporting affiliations. Hill 16 was taken over, becoming a second home for the new Dublin followers. The arrival of the team on the pitch, each and every score, every trophy presentation was greeted with a sea of blue. They called them "Heffo's Army" or just "The Dubs". Crowds of 30,000 turned up for league or first-round championship matches. More than 50,000 attended semi-finals. Gates exceeded 70,000 for championship deciders. It was a new phenomenon later replicated by Irish soccer supporters but never before seen in Gaelic football.

'What happened at the time was that the Dublin sporting public had nobody to follow,' Jimmy says. 'Drumcondra were gone out of the league and Shamrock Rovers weren't successful. A Dublin Gaelic football team came along and they decided to jump on the bandwagon. It was great for Gaelic football, not alone for Dublin but all over the country. It gave a new hype to the game. It was incredible.

'I used always say that I thought the fans enjoyed it more than we did. It seemed that every first round of the Leinster championship was played on the Whit Bank Holiday and it was always a glorious day. We'd go down to Tullamore or Portlaoise or Wexford and play a championship match. You'd be sweating in a cramped bus and you'd see the lads on the side of the road having their sandwiches and their pints and basking in the sun.

'They went down the country and they never created trouble. You got a number of odd-bods but that was inevitable given the number of people you had following Dublin. Even later on, in '83 when the replay of the All-Ireland semi-final was against Cork down in Cork, people said they were going to wreck the place yet that was one of the best weekends ever. They went down to Cork and they had a fantastic weekend with no trouble and no problems at all.

'During games you'd have huge support but you really wouldn't notice them. When you'd go out on the field you wouldn't notice them. Once the game started they disappeared until after the match. But they were the types of characters that always got on well with the team even when we got beaten. After games we'd go down O'Connell Street and they'd still turn out in their droves even when we were beaten in an All-Ireland final.

'I had good *craic* with the spectators. I'll always remember I got probably the biggest compliment I ever got in my life from this Dublin fellow. I was coming out of a match, probably just after '75 or '76, and I was going down to Meagher's pub to have a pint. He comes over to me down in Meagher's and he says: "Jem, do you know what? You gave me more out of life than me wife did." Now I never saw his wife and I don't even know whether he was married or not, but I think it was a compliment anyway.'

Any sport is guaranteed to flourish and thrive if it has two towering opponents boasting contrasting values and traditions. Like Muhammad Ali versus Joe Frazier or Steve Davis versus Alex Higgins, in the 1970s Gaelic football produced its own point of conflict in Dublin versus Kerry. It was a battle of city versus country, of city slickers versus culchies, of urban values competing with those from a rural landscape. For more than a decade the war raged, with the whole nation relishing the contests.

From the mid-1970s to the mid-1980s the rivalry between Dublin and Kerry filled the sporting press. In the early years Dublin ruled the roost, contesting six All-Ireland finals in a row, winning three. In time, Dublin's ageing team gave way to Kerry's bright young stars, who won seven out of the nine All-Ireland finals from 1978 to 1986. In all, from 1975 to 1985 both teams faced each other six times in All-Ireland finals. For the record, Kerry won five of those championship deciders and Dublin won once, although Dublin's 1977 semi-final victory over Kerry was regarded as just as vital as any championship title success. It was a passionate rivalry on the field of play but a friendly symbiosis off it.

'Kerry meant a terrible lot to us and I know we meant a terrible lot to Kerry,' Jimmy recalls. 'Over the years we've made a lot of friends out of it. Any time we're down in Kerry we'll have a drink with John O'Keeffe or Páidí Ó Sé or whoever. If they're up in Dublin we meet them and we have a few drinks with them. We built up a tremendous friendship.

'In '75 we just never got going. They were a crowd of young lads coming up from Kerry and we thought we were going to hammer them in Croke Park. We were roaring-hot favourites. We were too cocky going out on the field. Kerry got the breaks and they just totally caught us on the hop. Although we were getting to be an old team we were very determined to come back and win it in '76 and hope to play Kerry somewhere along the way, which did materialise.

'After beating Kerry in '76 we thought we'd broken Kerry's back. However, they came back in '77, in the All-Ireland semi-final, and people claim it was probably one of the best games ever played in Croke Park. As a player you wouldn't really know. Again we got the breaks. We got two goals near the end and we snuffed Kerry out. I think it was our determination that day not to be buried. A lot of teams going into the final quarter that day against Kerry would have thrown in the towel but we were determined not to throw in the towel.'

Having beaten Kerry in the 1977 semi-final, Dublin were left with the task of accounting for Armagh in the championship decider. That day Dublin were going for two-in-a-row. Armagh had arrived in the final following a tight one-point victory over Roscommon in their semi-final replay. Although Dublin were drained from their exertions against Kerry, they convincingly beat Armagh by a twelve-point margin, winning by 5–12 to 3–6. That was the day Jimmy Keaveney entered the record books for a 70-minute final with a personal tally of 2–6.

'It was a total anti-climax,' Jimmy says. 'Looking back on it, I feel sorry for Armagh. At no stage did it look like Armagh were going to beat us. Armagh had some fine players but it was just one of those days when Dublin were on fire and we scored at will. Even after the game everything was dead. Although we'd won an All-Ireland, everything was flat.

'A funny incident happened that particular day. My father, God be good to him, went to the match with my wife. We had only one child at the time, my daughter. I said to my father: "Look, we're parking the car at Clonliffe College. When the game is over, win or lose, I'll go up and I'll have a drink with you." He used to drink in a pub called the Comet on the Swords Road.

'When the game was over I told the lads I'd see them later on, got in my car, drove up, parked the car, went into the Comet and my father was there with a few friends. "Well done, Jimmy," they all said. I looked around and I saw my wife with an Armagh hat on her and my daughter with a little Armagh flag in her hand. "Jesus," I said, "what are you up to?" "Ah, well," she says, "you've won a couple already. It would be nice to see somebody else win it." That will give you an idea what she knows about Gaelic football.'

Following back-to-back victories in 1976 and '77, Dublin went for a three-in-a-row in 1978. Victory that day would have crowned a fantastic run of success stretching back to 1974. It all started so well, with Jimmy Keaveney scoring five points out of Dublin's opening six-point salvo. Kerry feebly responded with a single point. Then came John Egan's crucial goal followed by Mikey Sheehy's famous chip over Paddy Cullen's head. Dublin fell to pieces and, following an Eoin Liston hat-trick, were eventually crushed by 5–11 to 0–9. Despite the apparent rout, for Jimmy Keaveney 1978 was the match the Dubs let slip away.

'One final that I'm convinced to this day we should have beaten Kerry in was the '78 final,' Jimmy declares. 'We got a drubbing in the end but I remember in the first 15 minutes the Kerry defence were arguing. I think we were beating them by 0–6 to 0–1 and attacking and attacking. We were the team that was more likely to score a goal. We had them dead and buried. Unfortunately, a few of our own people, our own defenders, decided they wanted to go up and have a bit of the action, have a chance of scoring. We were caught with our trousers down. If we had held the head that day and if people hadn't got overconfident and if they had done what they were told to do, we would have won that All-Ireland.

'The first goal was by John Egan, who was probably the most underrated Kerry footballer ever. I had great time for John; he was a marvellous footballer. Mikey Sheehy and Eoin Liston did damage but overall John Egan did us more damage than the rest of them. Then came the famous chipped goal from Mikey Sheehy over Paddy Cullen's head and we were dead and buried. I think it should never have been allowed. Earlier on in the game I thought Paddy had fouled Ger Power but when he gave the free Paddy Cullen definitely did not foul Ger Power and when Mikey Sheehy took the free kick Séamus Aldridge wasn't even looking at it. He had his back to Mikey Sheehy. I don't think it should have been a free at all. If anything it should have been a free out for Dublin. The funny thing is that Mikey is famous for it and it made Cullen a millionaire. They were incidents that happened and they were all part and parcel of the fun. At the time it wasn't funny but when you look back it was a bit of *craic* anyway.

'After they beat us, I thought the bubble had burst. Going on to '79, I got put off in the Leinster final against Offaly and I got two months' suspension. We appealed it but it made no difference. The Pope was coming to Ireland in September of the same year so the All-Ireland final was brought back a week to facilitate the Pope. The suspension meant that I missed the All-Ireland semi-final and if we won that, which we did, then I missed the All-Ireland final. Really, the bubble had burst. The team were 34 or 35 years of age, not just one of us but about five or six of us, and we were sort of gone over the hill at that stage.'

In 1979 Jimmy Keaveney reached 34 years of age and was clearly in the twilight of his career. Remarkably, his revival in the Dublin shirt had only started back in 1974 when, at the age of 29, he won his first All-Ireland senior medal. In the intervening years he won two further All-Ireland senior medals in 1976 and '77 and two back-to-back Footballer of the Year awards in the same two years. Added to his three All-Star awards, it was a remarkable haul won in such a short span of time. It was only fair recompense for one of the finest finishers in the history of the game.

'I think it was just luck that Kevin Heffernan got together a successful Dublin team which basically, I would have said, was a rag-ball team,' Jimmy modestly concludes. 'He put a couple of young lads into it, he got a couple of big fellows to play and he moulded them into a very good team. Nobody else would have done it but Kevin Heffernan. We were all very average footballers. I really don't think we were an exceptional team but Heffernan made us into a good team.

'Mick O'Dwyer did the very same thing but I think Kevin did a better job than Mick because Mick had ready-made footballers from the Kerry team that had won U-21 All-Irelands. They were coming from a very successful background. We won damn all. I'm not saying anybody could have managed the Kerry team but it would have been a lot harder to do the job with Dublin than it would have been to do the job with Kerry.

'I enjoyed what we did, the fun and the *craic*. I don't mind about the medals; they're in the drawer somewhere in the house. At the end of the day it's not all about the awards and trophies you won but it's the friendships which make it great. I like all of the Dublin players, the Kerry players and the Cork players, the lot. I can go down to Cork and go to Kerry, go to the west of Ireland, go up to the north of Ireland and there will be somebody there that I know through football. This is the biggest kick I've got out of it anyway.'

8. JOHN EGAN

IN 1975 A BRILLIANT CORNER-FORWARD CAUGHT THE ATTENTION OF NATIONAL football audiences. A strong, intelligent player with a devastating turn of speed, he signalled his arrival in the big time with two goals against Tipperary in the first round of the championship. He scored two more goals against Sligo in the All-Ireland semi-final. Having already scored a crucial goal in the previous year's National Football League final, this extraordinary sharpshooter faced into the 1975 All-Ireland decider against Dublin as one of the aces in the new Kerry pack.

Although already an established Kerry senior player, it took until the 1975 All-Ireland final for the legend of John Egan to lift off. That day he tore Dublin apart. He scored a goal shortly into the game. He hit the crossbar with another goal-bound effort. It was from one of his passes that Ger O'Driscoll scored Kerry's second and decisive goal, finally putting the match beyond Dublin's reach. The 1975 All-Ireland final was a *tour de force* for John Egan, who secured his first All-Ireland senior medal while helping Kerry embark on their new golden era. A goal-scoring powerhouse of rare bite and quality had arrived on the football scene.

'I definitely was fortunate from the word go that any chance that came my way I seemed to be able to get goals,' John says. 'In '75 I seemed to get a goal in almost every round of the championship. I got a vital goal against Tipperary in the first round and two against Sligo. In the All-Ireland final we went into the game strangely enough feeling reasonably confident. Mick O'Dwyer had us flying, we feared nothing and our attitude on the day was perfect. It just so happened that Mikey Sheehy took a free and he miskicked it. He topped it and the ball flew in and it broke to me and I put the ball in the back of the net. That was vital for the team and it was vital for me and I think ever since I never had a fear of getting a goal against Dublin.

'I also hit the crossbar. The ball came through to me. Paddy Cullen is a big man, he came out and he spread himself. That time you could punch the ball into the net. I took the simple option and I said I'd punch it over his head, which I did. Everything was perfect, but the ball dropped down and hit the crossbar as it was dropping. If I had that chance again, I'd have booted it past him. You only get one chance and sometimes you score and sometimes you don't. I'm glad that wasn't a vital miss, it could easily have been. I definitely should have had another goal that day. I should have blasted that one to the net.

'Ger O'Driscoll then got a very good goal. There was a sweeping movement down the field. I think Ogie Moran played it to Ger Power and he played it to me. If you stop and think about it and adjust yourself, it's too late. Oftentimes you get a ball and you do the instinctive thing by whipping it across the square. I got that ball and I could see players coming in, so I turned and I just punched it. Ger O'Driscoll was flying in and he punched it into the net. It was a good, fast movement and a great finish by Ger. It was my beginning. I was delighted to have contributed so much in 1975. From there on then, I think every year after that I was always fortunate to get goals or create scores.'

Although eventually renowned as a corner-forward, the early signs were that John Egan's football prowess lay in entirely different sectors of the field. He began as full-back at U-14 level, moving eventually to centre-forward for his school and club. Strong and powerful, in time he graduated to the Kerry minors, where he became familiar to the public in a forward role. Despite defeat in the 1970 All-Ireland minor final, observers might have noticed some aspiring young names on that Kerry team. Among the names were Jimmy Deenihan, Mickey O'Sullivan, Ger Power and Paudie O'Mahony, not to mention the young John Egan. All those players, of course, would become stars in the years ahead.

Having progressed to the Kerry U-21s, John shared in the county's U-21 All-Ireland success in 1973. There, along with many of his former colleagues from minor level, he helped Kerry defeat

Mayo. Two years later, that achievement would be matched by another U-21 Kerry team containing players like Páidí Ó Sé, Charlie Nelligan, Ogie Moran, Pat Spillane and Mikey Sheehy. As those players progressed to the Kerry senior side, it was clear that something was about to happen. While all areas of the field were crammed with talent, tucked in at corner-forward was the powerful John Egan, known for his tight control, his solo runs and his coolness under pressure.

'I ended up being on the team as a corner-forward,' John recalls. 'I used to play outfield for my club and I always believed I was a better player if I was out centre-forward or somewhere like that. But I ended up getting on the team as a corner-forward and being a corner-forward is not an easy position to play. I know people would love to be getting goals and points and I suppose you could play corner-forward and you mightn't see an awful lot of the ball. You might get two chances, two balls with just the goalie to beat

'I definitely think one of the strengths I had as a corner-forward would be speed off the mark. I was very fast over ten yards or so. I was also very strong and I think strength is very important for inside-forwards because it's always going to be fairly physical there and the ball has to be won there. When I got to the ball I could shield it. People found it very hard to knock me off the ball. Once you got to the ball and you were strong and you had the ball in your possession, as a corner-forward you had all the options available to you then.

'One of my biggest assets would be having vision and passing the ball and moving it quickly. It can be too late if you don't see things faster than other people. Probably my biggest asset was having quick, incisive vision and being not afraid to pass. If I got a chance I wouldn't be afraid to take it on either. Even in the 1974 league final against Roscommon, they were a way better team than we were and they had us beaten off the park. They were up three points and the game was up. I didn't get a kick of the ball that day but I got a goal in the last minute and my name was all over the papers the following day. I think that's where the goal-scoring touch really started.

'In relation to the solo run, believe it or not I'm left-handed and right-footed. I used solo the ball off my right foot into my left hand and people thought it was a skill that I developed myself. You're covering the ball all the time; the ball is going across your body. I found that very useful because fellows didn't know which side the ball was going to be on. Maybe I'm a small bit ambidextrous as well in that I can move either way, either left or right, and I'm equally strong on both sides. I'm not necessarily as strong with my left foot as a kicker, but to be strong on one side is good enough once you can make space for yourself.

'Excitement or nerves never got to me even in big matches, which is a tremendous asset to have as well. When you look around the night before the match, some fellows are all nervous tension. You'd be woken on the Sunday morning with this fellow running up and down the corridor, with footballs hopping off walls and roofs and things like that. Some fellows would get very nervous to the point that you'd see them rushing in and out to the toilet and vomiting. The tension before big matches is something that's extraordinary. There's fierce tension and everybody suffers in different ways from it. I'd have to say personally that I was very lucky that nerves didn't bother me at all.'

Having won the National Football League in 1974, the Kerry machine was up and running. By now a wonderful set of young players had emerged from the Kerry minor and U-21 sides of the early 1970s. Devastating full-forward and half-forward lines were taking shape in the senior team. Players like Pat Spillane, Ogie Moran, Ger Power, Mikey Sheehy and John Egan were coming to the fore. They would soon be joined by the intimidating figure of Eoin Liston. In the meantime, the new Kerry senior team won their first All-Ireland title in 1975. Playing fluid, attacking football and coached by Mick O'Dwyer, a decade and more of Kerry dominance was about to unfold.

'Playing in that particular team starting in 1975, I'd have to say that the ball was always passed to a player in a better position,' John remarks. 'We kept moving the ball fast, which made us potent as a forward-line as distinct from being potent as individuals. Any time one of us got the ball we always played it to the guy in the better position. We built up confidence in each other and every player, to a man, had overriding personal confidence as well. If a chance came, it was taken. If there was a chance there to give it to another guy, he took it.

'All Mikey Sheehy, our bodyguard Eoin Liston and myself wanted inside was to get the ball in quickly to us. We were lucky in a sense that the three of us were totally unselfish to each other. We used always pass the ball and we always played as a unit. Everybody was moving quickly and when one or other had the ball other guys would move into space and the ball was played in fast. So we helped each other develop as well and we developed as a strong full-forward line because we all played together all the time.'

In 1978, boasting potent forwards like Mikey Sheehy, Eoin Liston and John Egan, Mick O'Dwyer's fledglings achieved their second championship triumph. Having lost to Dublin in the championship campaigns of 1976 and '77, Kerry powered past their rivals from Leinster to win the 1978 All-Ireland by the resounding score of 5–11 to 0–9. John Egan scored in every round of that championship campaign. Mikey Sheehy also scored his famous cheeky goal against Paddy Cullen in the championship decider. But, typically, it was one of Egan's golden goals that turned the All-Ireland final in Kerry's favour.

'Goals are very important,' John reflects. 'They turn the crowd with you and they turn the tide your way. That particular day, Dublin had us run off the field. They were winning by 0–6 to 0–1. I think it was Robbie Kelleher I was marking that day and I remember him going down to the other end of the pitch. I could have gone with him or I could have stayed where I was. If he had scored below at the far end and I had stayed where I was, I was in serious trouble. But I stayed where I was and the play broke down.

'The ball was moved up the field quickly and it came to Pat Spillane. I was unmarked inside because the corner-back had gone down the field. In fairness to Paddy Cullen, he came out very quickly. He came to smother me and I turned and played it over his head. That was another instinctive score. Definitely if I had dwelled on it that time he had me caught. I just took the first option I thought of and I threw it over his head. Thanks be to God, the ball hopped into the net. It was a vital score for us because our game was transformed after that.

'We all know Mikey's cheeky chip came shortly after. Ger Power backed into Paddy Cullen. A free was given to Kerry. It was a controversial decision and whether it was a free or whether it wasn't remains to be seen. But Mikey had extraordinary vision and quick thinking. If you saw Paddy Cullen and he trying to scurry back to the goal! It was a brilliant, brilliant score. It probably summed up Mikey Sheehy as much as anything else. Mikey was a fantastic, quick-thinking player, who always played the ball quickly to people. People still talk about that goal and they forget about my goal. We got two goals quickly in that game and I think that really finished the Dubs that day.'

With his love for the big occasion and his calmness under pressure, it was almost inevitable that John Egan would score another goal in the 1979 All-Ireland final. That was the day when the great Dublin team of the 1970s signalled their demise. It was also a day best remembered for Mikey Sheehy's brace of goals scored as part of his record-equalling tally of 2–6 for a 70-minute final. Not to be outdone, however, John Egan accounted for Kerry's third goal, which put paid to any hope Dublin might have of saving themselves from an embarrassing 3–13 to 1–8 defeat.

'It wasn't as vital as other goals but it really killed the game that day,' John remarks. 'It was a good goal in the sense that the ball came from Charlie Nelligan, who kicked this long kick-out. Mikey Sheehy fielded it, moved it on quickly to Jack O'Shea and he transferred it to me. Paddy Cullen came to me and again I had the option of punching the ball to the net, which was very useful for forwards at that time. I punched it under his body. That was a great team goal because the goal came all the way from one end of the pitch to the other. It was a very decisive score. Just talking of goals, a fellow said to me: "You know, Egan, you get a lot of lucky scores, you know, soft goals." "Well," I said, "whether they're soft or not, they're all vital." Would you believe it, I think a soft goal is nearly worth two goals at times.'

Having won his fourth and fifth All-Ireland senior medals in 1980 and 1981, John Egan went for medal number six in 1982. That year even the dogs in the street could tell you that Kerry would achieve their historic five-in-a-row. The only question was who from the Kerry panel would have the honour of captaining the side on this auspicious occasion? As it happened, the honour fell to John Egan. It turned out to be a dubious distinction, however, given the events that unfolded in Croke Park. There would be no victorious speech from the Hogan Stand by the Kerry captain. There would be no historic homecoming to Kerry with the Sam Maguire Cup. Instead, Kerry succumbed to Offaly by the score of 1–15 to 0–17.

'I think I was made captain by the toss of a coin,' John recalls. 'There was a bit of conflict and controversy between myself and Jack O'Shea over who should be captain. I won it on the toss and it was very important for the simple reason that a five-in-a-row was never achieved before. To look back on it now, on the game itself, it's extraordinary that we were four points up with about eight minutes to play and we lost the match. You'd feel beforehand that if you were four points up with eight minutes to play, you should be winning. We scored 0–17 in that game and lost. We missed a penalty but you can always miss a penalty. I wouldn't attribute missing the penalty as having anything at all to do with it. I'd say that we played too fine and we weren't tough or rugged enough. Offaly got a lot of points, they scored 1–15 and I think we gave them too much freedom around the pitch.

'Fellows say lots of things, including that our midfielders went back into defence and we got disorganised. But if you look back on it now, it was an extraordinary game. I remember Micheál O'Hehir saying at one stage: "There's a goal in this game yet." I think even he could see the tide was turning against us. Offaly were hungry and the longer they stayed in the game and as long as the game was close, they really believed they were going to beat us. If we had pulled four or five points clear of them, I think their heads might have gone down. But we left them in the game. I suppose what makes sport is that extraordinary things can happen. Nobody could have written the script for that in the sense that Kerry had the five-in-a-row wrapped up. It was in the bag and then it was just grasped away at the last minute.

'It was a heartbreaking defeat because of the manner in which we were beaten. Sometimes you're beaten and you can walk away and say: "Look, we were beaten." But the manner of that defeat was hard to take. I think we had a chance of winning it and we didn't win it and we'd have to say that Offaly played exceptionally well on the day. It was a great game of football and Offaly were brilliant. But as time passes and the years go by, it is then you feel how significant it would have been to have won the five-in-a-row. Maybe we could have won a five-in-a-row earlier. We could have won '77, '78, '79, '80 and '81 maybe, but we didn't. Having lost in '82, that was it and it possibly broke the sequence then.

'The team started breaking up a little bit after that and a few new fellows came in. We went down to Cork the following year and we didn't prepare particularly well for it. It was a thunder and lightning Munster final and we went into the game probably not really keyed up for it. Maybe it was a blessing in disguise that we lost. We lost by another last-minute goal. That was two years down the drain and two years in a player's career as he's getting older is an awful lot of time. I think that definitely broke the sequence of the great team. But that's the way it goes, as they say you can't win them all.'

Mick O'Dwyer's Kerry side got their second wind in the mid-1980s, when they won a further three All-Irelands in a row. John Egan shared in the first of those triumphs in 1984. Indeed, he contributed to Kerry's successful championship campaign that year by scoring another of his now-famous goals against Galway in the semi-final. By the time the championship had concluded, however, it was clear that the end of John's career had arrived. In 1985 and 1986 his colleagues Pat Spillane, Mikey Sheehy, Ogie Moran, Ger Power and Páidí Ó Sé went on to secure a further two All-Ireland medals, establishing a record of eight All-Ireland senior medals each. But John, who was there with Kerry that bit longer, had already retired, having accumulated six senior medals.

'We had lost in '83 and I took some time out,' John says. 'When you go over 30 and you start taking time out, it's like putting a good thoroughbred out in soft grass. You're inclined to soften up a bit. The rigours of training aren't there any more up to September. You're delaying training; you're putting it off and putting it off. Then you come back and you're doing these crash-courses in trying to get fit. Amazingly, you always have the ability and football never leaves you. But when your fitness goes and you're slower to the ball and you're getting cranky and you're not enjoying it any more, you just feel it's a chore.

'You have won it all and you're expected to win and when you start slipping at all and going downhill, hurlers on the ditch start talking. The confidence starts to leave you and you say to yourself: "Look, it isn't worth it any more." You're gone tired, in other words. You could definitely play on and on if you wanted to, but standards wouldn't be improving. There's a time for everything. It's sad to see very good players playing when they're old. I won't say they're disgracing themselves or anything like that, but you definitely can't compete with younger fellows as you get older.

'I just quit and I was delighted I made that decision. I quit club football and everything. Maybe a year after that you'd say: "Did I make the right decision or the wrong decision? Maybe I should still be playing." But I made the right decision and I'm delighted I made it myself. I didn't have to be told to go and I wasn't asked to go. In fact, Mick O'Dwyer came to me all that winter to know when I was getting back into shape. But I had a great innings and I'm delighted I made the decision.'

Throughout his career, John Egan became one of the most revered corner-forwards in the history of the game. He caught the eye despite being surrounded by so many other wonderful performers in Kerry's star-studded team. Although sometimes overlooked by commentators and critics, his standing amongst his peers is quite remarkable and his fellow-players repeatedly single him out for praise. Along with his six All-Ireland senior medals, he won four National Football Leagues, four Railway Cups and five All-Star awards. Beyond the silverware, however, the lasting and most potent memories he left behind may well be the powerful and devastating goals he scored for Kerry throughout their greatest-ever era.

'It's everybody's dream to get goals and to score in big matches and to get vital goals,' John concludes. 'I find it very hard to put my finger on why I was such a prolific goal-scorer. I definitely had to have a natural ability to take the opportunity when it arose, which I suppose is the most important thing for an inside-forward. I'm glad that they meant so much to my team and I'm glad that a lot of them were probably match-winning goals. We won't talk about the ones that I missed, only the ones that I scored. But it was a thrill for me to get goals and I suppose if it were nowadays, I'd have a fancy celebration like all of the soccer players. I'd love to be still scoring goals but I'm only scoring them in my dreams now. At least I can dream about the ones I got and not the ones that I might have got.

'I really enjoyed it. All these years later it's fantastic to see people watching the matches on television and still talking about us as a team. When we were playing we never realised how great we were.

We never realised the importance of it, how vital it was to other people as well, particularly people all over the world. We used to do a lot of travelling to America and England and you could not believe what representing your county and going out into Croke Park wearing the green and gold jersey meant to people there. People all over the world got so excited. When you won they celebrated with you and when you lost they were as disappointed as the players themselves. I definitely have to say that I was very lucky to have achieved what I achieved and to have played with a Kerry team that was so successful.'

9. BRIAN MULLINS

THERE ARE TWO CLASSIC CARTOON DRAWINGS DEPICTING THE CONTRADICTORY perceptions of a striker and a goalkeeper as a shot at goal is about to be taken. In the first drawing the striker sees the goalkeeper as massive, his huge frame obscuring all but a fragment of the net. In the second drawing the goalkeeper perceives himself to be tiny, a diminutive figure overshadowed by acres of net as he stands facing the striker. It's all a matter of perception; the same event viewed from two hugely different perspectives.

That stereotypical image of a striker overawed by the task ahead could never be applied to Dublin's Brian Mullins. For a start, he wasn't a striker at all but a midfielder known for attributes other than sticking the ball in the net. He was also part of a team with an abundance of goal-scoring talent. But on All-Ireland final day in 1976, against Kerry, he found himself faced with the job of slotting the ball past the goalkeeper. And the net didn't look tiny. In fact, all he could see was acres of net. There was no goalkeeper, no crowd, just vast swathes of netting waiting to welcome the ball.

'Part of the dream and fantasy that I used to indulge myself in when I was a young fellow was that I would score the winning goal in an All-Ireland final,' Brian Mullins says of that famous match-winning strike in 1976. 'I would go through in my mind the process of catching the ball, turning, beating one tackle and then bang! And there it happened. It actually happened for me. It happened so fast and in the spur of the moment that it was like as if God or somebody suddenly possessed me.

'When the opportunity came, I was nearly in some kind of a world that I was removed from. Suddenly, bodies fell and the goal opened up and I looked up to kick it into the net. It actually went in through Charlie Nelligan's legs, but all I could see was the net. The only analogy I can make is that I momentarily understood what a fish feels like when he finds himself just about to get stuck or caught in a net. It was just the whole area was net. I could see or witness nothing else other than net. It was amazing.

'It was only when the motion of moving and executing the kick and the ball ending up in the net was over and done that I realised: "God, you did it." I realised then that Kerry had been kind of coming back at us midway through the second half and this was a killer punch. This had put us back again into a comfortable lead zone. I realised the significance of it. But as it happened, although it was something that I always wanted to happen and hoped would happen, I couldn't believe it.'

Brought up in Dublin's Clontarf, Brian Mullins showed an appetite for Gaelic football from an early age. As a ten year old he was already playing in the local street leagues. He also benefited from the advice of his brother Seán, who played with St Vincent's and who coached his younger brother in the finer points of the game. In the 1970s Brian's rise was rapid. By the age of 16 he was making his first appearance as a minor with Dublin. 'I was sent off against Laois,' Brian recalls of the match. 'So if you ask can I remember my first outing with Dublin, I certainly can with honour and glory.'

In 1974, having caught the eye of Kevin Heffernan, Brian progressed to the Dublin senior football team, where he slotted into a side that would quickly become one of the finest in Gaelic football history. He made his début on Easter Sunday 1974 against a Sligo team containing Mickey Kearins. After that, a remarkable sequence of events unfolded. Dublin worked their way through Leinster, defeating a strong Offaly side on the way. They beat Cork in the All-Ireland semi-final. Then, on 22 September 1974 they beat Galway by 0–14 to 1–6 at Croke Park in the All-Ireland final. Brian Mullins, aged 19, had won his first All-Ireland senior championship medal.

'It was a magical moment,' Brian says. 'I would have had a dream and a fantasy pretending, as I was playing on the road and at various other venues, to be Mick O'Connell. I would be listening to Micheál O'Hehir and Micheál Ó'Muircheartaigh and hearing their commentaries and exclamations at the marvellous skills displayed by somebody. Then you'd go out and you'd try to replicate them yourself. You'd be talking to yourself as you were doing these skills and you were pretending that you were in Croke Park on All-Ireland day. And there I was. I was actually in Croke Park on All-Ireland day.

'I had sold programmes the year before and every year for donkey's years beforehand, as a lot of young Dublin fellows associated with clubs did. I sold programmes not only at All-Ireland finals but at all kinds of matches. So here I was out on the field and it was magical from that point of view. The other thing that crossed my mind was that if I won an All-Ireland medal I was going to give it to my mother. And there I was with my All-Ireland medal and I gave it to my mother and she wore it with pride and distinction. She handed it back to me a short while before she died.

'It was a big occasion and the fact that the fantasy of mine had come through to reality was absolutely amazing. It had a special place. You learn life lessons from sport and I learned an awful lot of life lessons during the first year. Certain standards and certain performances are promoted as being incapable of being mirrored or achieved by other people. But that year taught me that if you put your mind to it and you decide that there is something that you want to do then there's a fair chance that you are going to be able to do it. It taught me a lot in terms of life lessons like that.'

Nobody could have predicted the wave of hysteria that swept Dublin in the lead-up to the 1974 All-Ireland final. Hard-core Dublin supporters emerged from the woodwork after being dormant for decades. Committed GAA families found a focus for their sporting enthusiasm. New fans, transcending other sporting affiliations, were drawn to the game. Supporting the Dubs became fashionable across all social classes. In the years to come, an army of mobile fans travelled the country in support of their team. Croke Park was crammed when the Dubs played at home. Ticket fever gripped the capital. Gaelic football had never seen anything like it before.

The fans certainly had something to celebrate. It started with the All-Ireland victory in 1974. Then in 1975 the rivalry between Dublin and Kerry took off. Kerry won the first battle, securing the '75 All-Ireland title. The following year the tables were turned, with Dublin the victors. In 1977 came the classic semi-final between Kerry and Dublin, with Dublin progressing to a triumphant appearance against Armagh in the September decider. Gaelic football needed something like this. It was the rivalry of city versus country. It was also, in a sense, a metaphor for an Ireland that was divided between the urban metropolis of Dublin and the rest of the country. Whatever the cause of the upsurge in support, the phenomenon of 'The Super Dubs' had arrived.

'I've sometimes wondered about it myself, how it arose,' Brian says. 'It would appear that by either coincidence or divine intercession, we came just at the right time for the city and for a load of people who were crying out for something to associate themselves with. I'd say there was a strong element of coincidence in it. This great expression of support and joy manifested itself in the people of Dublin. They wanted to be associated with the team and they wanted to support us. I can't explain it really except that it was a social phenomenon of some description, which I don't fully understand. But in the housing estates and in the clubs scattered around Dublin there was a great momentum and spur given to all those people who had been possibly soldiering for years in promoting the games. A generation was born of youngsters, boys and girls, who considered it hip and popular and cool to be associated with supporting the team. From that point of view, it was definitely unique and sudden and quite tangible.

'It did have an impact on your private life and there were visible intrusions. I'm sure my family's lives were affected by it, by virtue of their association with me. It became impossible to have a sense of privacy. It became quite difficult to go out and have a quiet drink or to go to any place unnoticed. I wouldn't like to overstate that. It was still possible to have a life and to live life normally and it was nice. The one element of it that I took exception to and didn't like was the print media impact and I would take issue with some of the contents of headlines and of articles in papers that had a significant impact on me and my family. But I trusted in people's ability to separate fact from fiction or suggestion from reality, and in most cases that paid off.'

From 1974 to 1979 Dublin appeared in six successive All-Ireland finals, winning three. It was a remarkable run, especially considering the power of the Kerry team that provided the opposition in four of the finals and in one semi-final. Both teams were trained to the height of fitness. Both had an array of highly talented players. Both also were noted for their power in midfield. For Kerry, there was Jack O'Shea and Seán Walsh. For Dublin, there was Bernard Brogan and Brian Mullins. Driven and inspired by Kevin Heffernan, the Dubs were a partly effective antidote to a Kerry team that threatened to pulverise all before them in the quest for All-Ireland glory.

'The only way I can describe what we were about is that we were about ambition,' Brian remarks. 'We were about a time in life, about achieving when you had the opportunity and when you could. We were about competition, about man pitted against man within the confines of the rules of the game. There's no doubt that Kevin Heffernan generated and engendered in us a tremendous sense of spirit and of doing ourselves justice. He had a sense of it being a team sport, we were all in this together and there was a way that we should carry ourselves in trying to deliver on our goals and our ambitions. He was excellent at getting into the minds of individuals and then developing the individual thought-process into the team ethos.

'A dressing-room of a team is a very interesting place to be. Nerves and tensions manifest themselves in different ways in people. Kevin had to try and co-ordinate all the different nervous dispositions and get them on to the one track. He did that. He was brilliant at that. He was also brilliant at identifying what it was that made each individual click; what he had to say to each individual and in some circumstances what he didn't say to individuals that made it work for them, he was excellent at that. He created in us a great sense of belonging, of group dynamics, loyalty to the cause, concentration and effort, and that you're only as strong as your weakest link.

'My role was made up of two main things. One was to try to create a dominance in terms of winning possession and ensuring that as much of it as possible went towards the goal we were trying to score in as opposed to the goal we were trying to defend. The second thing was to minimise the pressure that I allowed come on to our forwards or our backs. I would see it from both those points of view. The midfield position gave me great liberty. As a corner-back you don't have much liberty to head off and do your own thing. Your first and foremost duty is to try and make sure that your man does as little as possible in terms of scoring and winning possession and setting up other scores. But out in the middle of the field you don't have to be so conscious of who you're marking, even though at times you do have to attend to making sure that your direct opponent is being dominated or competed against. From that point of view I had a certain sense of freedom. But then the midfield role in terms of being available for kick-outs from both ends of the field, as a link between the backs and the forwards, as a contributor to the way forwards attack and to the way defenders defend, was an important role as well.'

In 1974, '76 and '77 Brian Mullins won three of his four senior All-Ireland medals. Remarkably, he was only 22 years of age at the time he won his third. National Football League victories also added to his medal collection. By 1979, however, the Dubs had suffered two successive All-Ireland final losses to Kerry and it was clear that the team were beginning to fade. No one, however, could have predicted what would happen next to Dublin's star midfielder, Brian Mullins.

In late June 1980, Brian was travelling on Dublin's Clontarf Road when he almost lost his life. He had returned from a holiday in Wexford for training with Dublin. It was late at night. While driving along the Clontarf Road he was blinded by on-coming headlights and his car went out of control. He wasn't wearing a seatbelt. His car crashed into a lamppost. Brian ended up in the back of the car, suffering a serious fracture to his femur along with many cracked bones in his skull. He was lucky to survive what seemed to be a career-terminating accident.

'Simply put, I had an argument with a concrete lamppost and the concrete lamppost won, but that's probably too dismissive a remark,' Brian recalls. 'I was holidaying in Wexford with Helen and the children. It was a Friday evening and I had told Kevin that I would come up for the weekend for training and for a match. I drove up to Dublin on the Friday afternoon and the county final was on in Croke Park. A few colleagues that I knew were going to that, so I went too. After the match finished in Croke Park at maybe half-eight or nine o'clock, they adjourned to a hostelry in town and I could see that a heavy drinking session was starting, so I left.

'I started driving towards Portmarnock, where I was living, and I started driving too fast. I put the boot down out the Clontarf Road. At this stage, it was dark and I was blinded by a set of headlights coming the other way. Instead of keeping my eyes on the road, I covered my head with my hand and my arm and turned my head wrongly. The car veered the other way and the next thing I saw was a lamppost coming directly at me. At this stage, I was doing about 50 or 60 miles an hour and the next thing I woke up in the car and I didn't know where I was. One of the many things that I found out later was that the lamppost that I saw and the lamppost that I hit were about 200 metres apart. So something knocked me out in the initial stages of the trauma, either my head hitting the steering wheel when the car hit the kerb or something like that.

'I wasn't wearing a seatbelt, although I would always wear a seatbelt and I would advise anybody to wear one. It was a small Fiat belonging to my brother that I was driving and I was just fluked. Maybe it was the way God was looking after me. I ended up in the back of the car and the driver's seat was demolished. The concrete lamppost was where the driver's seat was, touching the gear stick. If I had been wearing a seatbelt I definitely wouldn't have survived, so I was fortunate that I wasn't wearing one.

'I had a lot of facial injuries because of whatever smack my head got. Of course, I would have had bruises and cuts all over. But the other major injury was that I had fractured mid-shaft the femur bone on my right leg, which is the bone between your hip and your knee. The danger was that if they tried to plate it or pin it, the risk of infection was far higher. So they decided to maximise the potential for not getting infection into my bloodstream and they put me on what's known as traction. Traction meant that I was tied to the bed for a long period of time and was uncomfortable. In that context, the wastage of muscle is tremendously enhanced. But if your bone succeeds in throwing up enough callus it's a better way to go. Thankfully, mine healed.

'I spent somewhere between six and eight months in and out of hospital and everything else. I was lucky, very fortunate that I got through it. I'm blessed with tremendous healing, which you inherit from your parents, and I had the best of medical care in the Mater. My surgeon did great work for me, particularly in relation to my leg which was shattered. I thankfully got back in two years to being able to walk, jog and subsequently run. I was very, very lucky from that point of view.'

Following a long and protracted struggle to regain fitness, Brian Mullins made a remarkable return to the Dublin team, where he once more slotted in at midfield. It says something for his dogged perseverance that he not only recovered his ability to play football again but that he did so at the highest level. Remarkably, the new-look Dublin team he returned to battled their way to the 1983 All-Ireland final, where they defeated Galway by 1–10 to 1–8. Unfortunately for Brian, he was sent off following an altercation with Brian Talty, becoming one of four players to receive their marching orders in a controversial and bad-tempered game. The victory in 1983 secured him his fourth All-Ireland medal.

'To be sent off in an All-Ireland final in front of a crowd and with all my family there, and having got back to where I was, it was a tremendously saddening experience,' Brian reflects. 'It kind of brings you down to earth when you sit back and you try to analyse it. After sitting in the dressing-room afterwards when all the hullabaloo had died down and everybody was gone, I went home. I didn't even go anywhere. I just went home to the house and I couldn't believe it had all transpired so quickly. A football match is a short time, in many circumstances, and things happen. Before you know it, it's over and done and dusted. You can't change it. I remember thinking to myself: "Is this a dream? Is this a bad dream? Am I going to pinch myself and wake up and it will only be the night before the match?" To be sent off in an All-Ireland final was, I am loathe to use the word depressing, but it was a tremendously saddening experience.'

In 1984 and '85 Brian Mullins and the Dublin team returned to Croke Park, where they suffered two successive All-Ireland final defeats to Kerry. The new Dublin team of the 1980s was running out of steam. Their midfielder Brian Mullins had been giving his all to the side for more than a decade and his days clearly were numbered. The ravages of Dublin's long odyssey, not to mention the atrocious injuries received in the car crash, were beginning to take their toll. Significantly, Brian was taken off in the 1985 final. Although just heading into his 30s, the end of his playing career was in sight.

In early 1986 Kevin Heffernan brought his inspirational reign as Dublin manager to a close. Into his place stepped a joint-management team consisting of Robbie Kelleher, Seán Doherty and Brian Mullins. It didn't last long, however, with Mullins leaving the post later that season. In the 1990s he had a spell managing Derry. But it wasn't for his forays into management that Brian Mullins would be recalled in the years ahead. Instead, whenever mention is made of Dublin's greatest years the image arises of this towering midfielder, with his remarkable fielding skills and his accurate passing. A powerhouse at the centre of Dublin's great team of the 1970s, Brian Mullins was the mainstay of a side that enriched football but may well have under-achieved in the process of doing so.

'We should have won in '78,' Brian says in conclusion. 'We shouldn't have allowed the three-in-a-row opportunity to disappear. I think '78 would have been the big one that we should have and could have won. Maybe '79 also. But regarding '75, I don't think we would have been back in '76, '77 and '78 if it weren't for losing '75 because we learned a huge lesson that year. So '78 definitely and maybe '79 would be two that I would regret. That's if I have regrets and I've no right to have regrets. In the 1980s, when there was the new team, we went on to the next phase of it. We played Kerry in '84 and '85 and I feel that maybe one or two of those we could have won. But if I were to look back on it I would see '78 as being a watershed.

'My primary emotions looking back on it would be how lucky and fortunate I was, how tremendously exciting and interesting it was and a great sense of the energy of it. The strength and the health that I had were a great plus for me, particularly in circumstances where players who suffered soreness and injuries would either miss training or subsequent matches. I rarely, if ever, missed anything over an injury or soreness. Some people used to joke that I never ran fast enough to suffer a soft tissue injury, but I used to take that with a lump of salt.

'They were great times. I mean, my older brother Seán played with Dublin for years during the 1960s and early '70s, with Tony Hanahoe, Jimmy Keaveney, Gay O'Driscoll, Paddy Cullen, Seán Doherty. He decided to stop when he was about 28 or 29 because he got a job in Portlaoise, in the County Council, and within a year or 18 months we had won an All-Ireland and I was only 19. There's very little else that you can use as an analogy to outline how fortunate I believe I was. I had great people who, at the right time, used to say: "Come on, Brian, you can do this, come on!" But out in the game, in the arena, in the cauldron of sport, you have to stand up and be counted. You're the one who has to do what's required to be done at the appointed time. That's great not only for sport but for life as well, and I have great memories of things like that.'

10. EOIN LISTON

NO OTHER FULL-FORWARD IN THE HISTORY OF GAELIC FOOTBALL BROUGHT A MORE convincing image to the role than Kerry's Eoin Liston. A giant of a man with a massive frame, he destroyed opposing defences with his strength and skill. Defenders dreaded marking him. Few goalkeepers relished the prospect of facing him in a league or championship game. Whether he was scoring crucial hat-tricks, as he did in the 1978 All-Ireland final, or whether he was feeding his fellow Kerry forwards with perfect passes, Eoin dominated attack like no full-forward before or since.

From his arrival in the senior squad in 1977, 'Bomber' Liston proved to be the missing link in Kerry football. With Eoin alongside Mikey Sheehy, Ogie Moran, John Egan, Ger Power and Pat Spillane, the Kerry forwards were as perfect as any forward-line could ever be. Their options seemed limitless. Among them were inch-perfect lay-offs from Liston. Alternatively, there were Liston's massive bursts of speed followed by his powerful shots at goal. When things got desperate, high balls lobbed in to Eoin could turn a game. The truth is, however, that things rarely turned desperate for this famous Kerry side.

'I played a lot of basketball at under-age level and I think that helped a lot,' Eoin says regarding his multipurpose full-forward role. 'Gaelic football is a team game and you're passing a lot. It isn't who scores; you're setting up other fellows. It never really bothered me whether I was scoring or who was scoring. It was kind of a reflex action. If I caught a ball and saw a fellow moving, the obvious thing without even thinking was to throw it to the person that I felt was moving into a good position. That was part of my game and Mick O'Dwyer always encouraged it. He didn't like selfish players and he always recognised in me that my play was unselfish. That's what teamwork was all about and once it was recognised by the coach we were going to keep doing it. Once Kerry were winning that was all that mattered to us.

'I was very lucky with so many players like Mikey Sheehy and John Egan alongside me and Ogie outside and Pat Spillane and Ger Power. It was easy to play with that forward-line. If I had an off-day today then Spillane might be Man of the Match. If Spillane had an off-day maybe Ogie was Man of the Match. We weren't just relying on one or two players. Everyone rowed in and if one fellow wasn't up to scratch, someone else took over that day.

'We had a midfield with Seán Walsh and Jack O'Shea, which was a superb partnership. We also knew how good our backs were. I often think they didn't get enough credit. Even today in soccer it's the forwards who get all the glory but we had some brilliant defenders like John O'Keeffe. He gave me more roastings night after night after night in training, which helped me as a footballer. When you're in there and playing at a top level night after night marking a fellow like John O'Keeffe and you're getting roasted, you have to work hard at your game. You have to try out new things and try to develop a few little tricks. You wouldn't work as hard if you were winning inside in training.

'We had Páidí Ó Sé, Tim Kennelly, Jimmy Deenihan and Paudie Lynch, who was a superb player and could do everything with the ball. Most of those players were able to play midfield at club level, which is a good test of backs. You've got to be a good footballer to play midfield and every one of that back-line could play midfield with their clubs. It will tell you what good footballers they were. I was lucky to come on at that time with so many good players around.

'If I was to try and analyse my own game a bit, I think I was fast for a big fellow. If I was marking a big fellow I always felt that I had the speed over him. I wouldn't be a speed-merchant by any means but I'd be fast for a big fellow, if you understand what I mean. If the ball was played out right or left, I'd usually be out first to it. I didn't like marking small fellows because they were usually speedier and faster than me. However, if I was marking a small fellow I felt I had an advantage if the ball was kicked in high. As a full-forward you're totally dependent on the quality of ball you get in and I was lucky enough with Jacko and Seánie delivering balls in from midfield. They knew where to put them to give me the advantage and that's what it's about really as a full-forward.'

Brought up in Ballybunion, Eoin Liston took an early shine to soccer, which he and his friends played on the local beach. Eoin soon received a nickname borrowed from a popular and stocky centre-forward who played for Bayern Munich. Like his namesake, who scored over 600 career goals, including 68 for West Germany, Liston would in time become a prolific target-man and sharpshooter for his team. Both players possessed an appetite for rattling the net while sharing an astonishing ability to pick up silverware. The original source of Eoin's nickname was the victorious World Cup star and triple European Cup winner – Gerd 'Bomber' Müller.

'The first time I was called "Bomber" was in a soccer match down on the beach in Ballybunion,' Eoin recalls. 'We used to play regularly down there. Back around the early '70s Gerd Müller was a lazy fellow who used to hang around the box and score a few goals. I used to hang around the square as well. I think a few of my mates down the beach reckoned that my work-rate wasn't up to it and they started calling me "Bomber". I've had it a long time.'

From the moment he arrived on the Kerry football scene, Eoin Liston left his mark. Having caught Mick O'Dwyer's eye while playing for the Kerry U-21s, he was soon elevated to the senior team, where he arrived just in time to see his county lose their second crucial championship match in a row to rivals Dublin. 'There was a lot of desperation in Kerry,' Eoin says of those defeats by Dublin in the All-Ireland final of 1976 and the semi-final of 1977. 'They were going to have one last shot at it to try and beat this great Dublin team.'

With the core of a fine side already in place, Mick O'Dwyer added some final touches to his Kerry team for the 1978 championship. Already in position were powerful players like Mikey Sheehy, Pat Spillane, Ger Power, Ogie Moran and John Egan. With the arrival of 'Bomber' Liston came the final missing link. In the 1978 Munster final, Eoin played a starring role as Kerry beat Cork by 3–14 to 3–7. In the All-Ireland final what better opponents could they face than the old enemy, Dublin?

That All-Ireland final day in 1978, John Egan stemmed Dublin's initial onslaught with a crucial goal in the first half. It was also the famous day when Mikey Sheehy chipped Paddy Cullen with his controversial goal just before the break. However, from Eoin Liston's point of view it's best remembered for his historic hat-trick of goals scored in the second half. Those three goals dumped Dublin's dream of three successive championship victories over Kerry onto the football scrap heap. For the record, Kerry crushed Dublin by 5–11 to 0–9.

'There was a big build-up to that match,' Eoin recalls. 'We really knew that Dublin had a great team but from training I felt Kerry had a great team too. I said: "They must be very good if they can beat us." I remember feeling like that at the time. Next thing, in the All-Ireland final we were 0–6 to 0–1 down and it looked like there was only one team on the field. I remember saying to myself: "God, they are a brilliant team, this Dublin team."

'It was a very funny, unusual game in that it took a bit of a twist with about three or four minutes to go before half-time. We got a great goal against the run of play. All of a sudden I remember Mikey Sheehy chipping Paddy Cullen. From us playing useless for one half, we went in ahead at half-time. We felt that we had to win this game at that stage. We had got every break. We hadn't even started playing and here we found ourselves ahead. In the second half, things went well for us and we won well in the end.

'At the time, all we were interested in was winning the match. The most important thing for any fellow in Kerry is to win an All-Ireland medal. There's fierce pride in the county, pride in the jersey and there's a sense of achievement if you're the holder of an All-Ireland medal. I think the first one is the most important one to any player. You feel that you've achieved something here in Kerry that's well respected. That's all that was in our heads at the time. If we could beat that Dublin team and get one All-Ireland medal, that was all we were looking for. We were absolutely delighted to achieve it.'

The victory over Dublin in 1978 launched Kerry and Eoin Liston on a four-year run of championship success. Kerry replaced Dublin as the form team of the years ahead. By 1978 the great Dublin team of the 1970s was already in decline. Players like Jimmy Keaveney, Tony Hanahoe and Paddy Cullen were over 30 while others were approaching the crucial 30 mark. The Dublin–Kerry rivalry continued, however, into 1979 when both sides squared up to each other in the championship decider. Reflecting Kerry's rise and the Dubs' decline, the Kingdom won that contest by 3–13 to 1–8.

'Dublin had a great team at that time,' Eoin remarks. 'They were in six different All-Ireland finals from '74 up to '79. They had some brilliant players. Have no doubt about it, they brought huge interest back to the game in Dublin and all over Ireland. There was a kind of city versus country thing and a lot of the counties would have been cheering for us at that time, with us being the country boys against the crowd from the city. But there was a great friendship built up out of that rivalry.

'There was no friendship at the time; they were winning the medals and getting the trips to San Francisco and we weren't. We were trying to bring a bit of pride back to Kerry and it was very important for us to do that. Having said that, they brought a new level of marketing to the game, which was badly needed, and it helped our profile then because we were getting great plaudits for beating them in the '78 and '79 All-Irelands. I think the level of interest really increased around that time.'

There was no doubting the impact of Eoin Liston on Kerry's revival in the years following 1978. As a sharpshooter his contribution was immense. He scored two crucial goals against Cork in the 1980 Munster final. He grabbed three against Clare in the 1981 Munster championship. He scored further goals against Mayo in the 1981 championship semi-final and against both Clare and Armagh in 1982. His reputation as a deadly striker was assured.

Equally crucial were Eoin's distribution and allocation skills, passing and flicking balls to natural predators like Pat Spillane, Mikey Sheehy, John Egan and Ogie Moran. Broadcast commentaries described passing movements from Liston to Spillane to Sheehy to Egan, or any combination thereof, and ending with the ball in the back of the net. He was a marvel at linking with his fellow-forwards, drawing them into the game, catching balls from high in the air and passing them to his Kerry colleagues. Observers marvelled at how such a towering, well-built man, with limited natural fitness and no great love of training, could master his skills so well.

'I was teaching down in Waterville at the time,' Eoin says. 'That's where Micko was from so I was with him, I'd say, five or six days a week. I was lucky enough. He was training me even on the days that he wasn't training Kerry. We used to play golf together, we used to play handball together; we'd play a load of different sports. He'd call for me and I had no choice only to go for a run with him. The nights that we were off I didn't go for a run. I knew I would train twice as hard the next day. In fairness, he could see that I didn't like training too much and he sat on top of me and made sure that I got out and built my fitness up to a level that I never thought I could reach and wouldn't have reached only for him. He's a great friend of mine today, a super man. I've great respect for him, always had, and I think all the players had. If you have respect for a coach like that you'll keep digging deep into yourself when the pain is there. You won't quit because you have a certain loyalty to your coach. We certainly had that for Mick O'Dwyer.'

In 1980 and 1981 Mick O'Dwyer's superb Kerry team powered their way to two further championship titles. They narrowly beat Roscommon in 1980 by 1–9 to 1–6, with Eoin Liston an unfortunate spectator at the match. 'I had appendicitis,' Eoin explains. 'About the Tuesday night before the match I was in training and wasn't feeling that well. Coming home in the car I was very sick. I went to the doctor and he sent me straight in to have my appendix taken out. I think it was on the Wednesday morning that I had the appendix operation, so I missed the final.'

The following year Liston was back in blistering form, scoring a personal tally of 3–3 in Kerry's championship rout of Clare. He scored a further 1–2 in the All-Ireland semi-final victory over Mayo. He then shared in Kerry's success over Offaly in the championship decider. That day, 20 September 1981, Kerry achieved a famous and historic four-in-a-row. The Kingdom had rarely witnessed euphoria quite like it in the county's long and distinguished football history.

'I hadn't experienced losing at the time,' Eoin says. 'My very first championship we won the All-Ireland. My second one we won. The third one we won and here we were going for a four-in-a-row. I hadn't experienced what it was like at that stage to lose a championship. We couldn't see ourselves being beaten at the time. I think the senior players on the team, the Jimmy Deenihans, John O'Keeffes, Paudie Lynchs, they knew from losing to Dublin in '76 and '77 exactly how it felt. They kept us motivated and focused and made sure that we didn't drop our guard. In 1981 we had a great campaign, we had a great match, a good final with Offaly and that was when we won the four-in-a-row.

'It was great to win. There was a great buzz around the place. We'd come home to Kerry and the first day we'd usually come to Killarney. Then we'd go to Tralee the following night. Then we'd go to the captain's home club on the Wednesday night and then we'd go down to Mick O'Dwyer's on the Friday night. There was a lot of drinking going on at the time, a lot of celebrating. Among the players there was a great friendship, a great bonding and we enjoyed each other's company. We enjoyed every bit of *craic* that went with it. We'd have Listowel Races and the players from the beaten county would usually come down. The Dubs were often down and we made friendships that would last for life. It's the memories of that and the memories of the trips abroad that are important and stick out.'

The story of Kerry's failed quest for a remarkable five-in-a-row in 1982 is often lamented in the pubs of County Kerry. Mikey Sheehy's penalty miss is ruefully recalled. Séamus Darby's goal at the death is grimly remembered. That Offaly won by a single point and a final score of 1–15 to 0–17 is almost unbearable. Even harder to stomach is that awful sense of shock, that feeling of deflation so at odds with the Kingdom's pre-match confidence that history was about to be made.

'We didn't think we were going to be beaten,' Eoin recalls. 'There was a lot of hype. Everybody was talking about making history and T-shirts were out with "Five-in-a-Row". Mick O'Dwyer, in fairness to him, was trying to say: "Look, it's just another game, we've been here before." I don't think we lost our focus. We prepared very hard for that match but I must give credit to Offaly. Even the year before, in '81, it was a super game we had with them and they nearly pipped us. In the semi-final the year before that we had an excellent game with them, which I think was something like 4–15 to 4–10, a great scoring game with good sets of forwards on both sides.

'If you look at that Offaly team under Eugene McGee, he had brought them a step further for six years. He had got them to the final for the second year running. He had lost the final the year before. He had lost the semi-final the year before that. He had lost the Leinster final the year before that again. He'd got a step further every time and he studied our game and he learned. He's an excellent coach. He's a lovely man with a great knowledge of the game. I've no doubt that he looked at and studied our game and he saw weaknesses. He exploited those weaknesses, which any good coach would try to do. It was a good Offaly team. There was a lot of good players on that team and it was no fluke that they beat us.'

In the following years Kerry and Eoin Liston battled their way to a further three All-Ireland titles, with all three remarkably won in succession. He played in Kerry's victories over Dublin in 1984 and 1985. In 1986 he shared in the Kingdom's triumph over Tyrone. His power and strength as a player also attracted the attention of a rugby league club in the UK, which toyed with the idea of hiring his services.

'I remember I played against Dublin, in '84 I think, and I made an awkward tackle on Ciarán Duff under the Hogan Stand. I ran into him and flattened him and some journalist printed something in the paper about this fellow, "Bomber" Liston, who was 16 stone and could do the 100 metres in 10.01 seconds or something like that. It was way off the mark. I got a phone call anyway from some rugby league club. Their team coach was reading the paper and picked this up and rang me to know if I'd come over for a trial.

'I said: "Do you realise what you're dealing with here? I can't run the 100 metres in 10.01 or 11.01 or 12.01." He said he'd be interested in doing it as an experiment and he was flying my wife and I over. I said: "If you want to do an experiment, I'll go for the week, no problem." Funny enough, that day at a club match I pulled a hamstring. I rang him back and said: "Look, I've a hamstring gone. I'm out for three or four weeks. You'll be wasting your money." So it never materialised.'

During his last years with Kerry, Eoin Liston remained a dominant presence. He continued to score crucial goals and points and he never relinquished that unselfish role of team provider that marked him out from the start. However, a strong Cork team was coming to the fore in Munster and it blocked Kerry's advance out of the province for the four years from 1987 to 1990. Kerry's great era was over and it took until 1997 for the county to once more win an All-Ireland title.

Eoin Liston formally retired in 1990 but made a brief return to the Kerry fold a few years later. Asked by his friend Ogie Moran to try one more shot in the Kerry shirt, he couldn't resist the temptation. It was a short-lived re-acquaintance with his county, however, and the end was clearly in sight. Having straddled three decades of Kerry football, 'Bomber' Liston finally hung up his boots and departed the game with his many medals and awards, the most important of which were his seven senior All-Irelands and his four All-Star awards.

'I was losing interest,' Eoin recalls. 'Your focus changes, you're getting older and you're more mature. You're settling down and raising a family. You think you're giving the same commitment to the football but you're not really. I was putting on weight and eventually I decided to call it a day after 1990. Then a friend of mine, Ogie Moran, became trainer in '93 and asked me if I'd have one go to see if I could get in shape again just for one year. He told me: "I'll tell you if I don't think you're up to it." It was an experiment and I was glad at the time.

'I have absolutely great memories of it all and I still love the game today. I can go up the road and see two U-16 teams playing and get great fun out of watching that match even if I don't know any of the players. I'm just delighted to have been playing at a time when Kerry had great success and we travelled the world. I've been to Australia twice and travelled to America 20 or 30 times. I've seen the world. I'm very much indebted to the GAA and to the people that have put in great work at under-age level to get us up to the level that we reached. I enjoyed every bit of it, enjoyed every celebration that went with it and made great friends out of it. They were great days and for anyone looking back they're the memories that you want – memories of the friends you make and the fun you've had.'

11. MIKEY SHEEHY

ALL-IRELAND FINAL DAY, 24 SEPTEMBER 1978, WILL BE REMEMBERED FOREVER AS A landmark in Gaelic football history. That day Kerry beat Dublin to win their twenty-fourth championship title. Dublin were denied a famous three-in-a-row. Eoin Liston scored a hat-trick. John Egan also rattled the net. Kerry goalkeeper Charlie Nelligan was sent off. Pat Spillane was Man of the Match. Nothing, however, compared with the moment shortly before half-time when Mikey Sheehy pulled from his conjurer's hat one of the most controversial and sensational goals ever scored at Croke Park.

The event has been seared into national memory. Dublin goalkeeper Paddy Cullen was adjudged to have fouled Kerry's Ger Power. A free was given, perhaps unfairly. Cullen, who was out of his goal, argued his innocence. Incensed and indignant, he remonstrated with referee Séamus Aldridge. Mikey Sheehy advanced. Dublin's Robbie Kelleher innocently gave him the ball. Cullen spotted the impending danger and backtracked. He was too late, however, as Sheehy's quickly taken shot dropped into the net. It was game, set and match as Dublin crumbled, Kerry stormed to victory and Mikey Sheehy's name entered folklore for the cheekiest goal ever scored in Gaelic football history.

'I've seen it in slow motion, fast motion, every motion,' Mikey says of that famous chipped goal. 'Ger Power and Paddy Cullen had a couple of incidents early on and they got to know each other. I'd say Ger followed through on Paddy at one stage and Paddy kind of followed through on him at another stage. The crowd knew that there was a bit of banter going on between the two of them but there certainly was no free. I've seen it many times on television since and Paddy did absolutely nothing wrong. He was perfectly entitled to ask Séamus Aldridge what the free was for.

'I went over to Robbie Kelleher to get the ball off him and he literally just handed the ball to me. He more or less gave it to me. What was obviously going through my head was to try to take the chance and get a goal. It was just one of those things. I saw a bit of a gap and it went in. I looked to see was it being allowed. The umpire waved the green flag and Séamus Aldridge went out the field. When we were inside in the dressing-room at half-time Mick O'Dwyer never said a word about it. I've always felt to this day that if I'd missed it I would have been shot because he would have felt that it was an easy enough chance for a point. After the game he said it was OK, it was a good goal but he never said a word at half-time.

'It was an important score in that it was close enough to half-time. It certainly had a bearing on the game because a lot of the Dublin lads went in at half-time with their heads down and they were shocked. Dublin were in total control early on in that game and they led us by 0–6 to 0–1. John Egan got a goal maybe about 10 minutes before my goal, which got us going. We'd been playing very poorly up to then and we had lost our shape. I won't say that Dublin felt that the game was won but they kind of started playing exhibition football. I remember early on Robbie Kelleher was marking me and we were at the Canal End. I'd say he ended up around Hill 16 at one stage. He was playing left corner-back and he ended up in the wing-forward position for the Dubs. When John Egan got the goal, their defence was caught out because they were all out the field. When that goal went in I felt there was a higher step in our stride afterwards. That had a bigger bearing than my goal.

'If I were to get a penny or a cent nowadays for every time I'm asked about that goal I'd be a wealthy man. Sometimes I actually get fed up talking about it. Anywhere I go someone will mention it, so I can imagine how poor Paddy feels when he's asked about it. Paddy is a great character and we've become great friends. We have often sat down, had a couple of pints and had a chat over it. In fairness to him, when he had his pub in Ballsbridge he asked me would I give him the boots that I wore that day, which I did, and he had them behind the bar. We are great friends and he's very jovial. I think he was what the GAA needed at that time. He was a flamboyant goalkeeper, a brilliant goalkeeper, he was a great showman and a great character.'

By the time of Kerry's remarkable win in 1978, Mikey Sheehy was blossoming into one of the finest strikers in the history of Gaelic football. Very few players could even approximate the attacking skills he possessed. He was, quite simply, the ultimate sharpshooter. Perfectly built, he exuded confidence and had marvellous balance and control of the ball. Like all great strikers, he had that uncanny knack of being in the right place at the right time. With an unerring nose for goal, he always sensed the chance to score. Inevitably, Mikey Sheehy would chalk up massive scores at the height of Kerry's glory years.

'Our house was a gable-end house,' Mikey recalls of his years growing up in Tralee. 'There was the back entrance door, which I used to open, and that was my target. I used to spend hours practising there. I also had the chimney area for a target, which was up higher. It was a cemented little area and I used to be practising against that from every side. My mother used to be giving out to me because the front door was from a very tight angle and I used to be having pot-shots in there as well. Unfortunately, there were a few windows broken. I used to spend hours and hours there kicking a ball. That's where I started playing football and I suppose all that probably helped later on when my career took off.'

At minor level in the early 1970s, Mikey Sheehy twice finished up on the losing end to Cork teams boasting promising players like Jimmy Barry-Murphy. At U-21 level, Kerry performed better. Players like Pat Spillane, Ger Power, John Egan, Jack O'Shea, Ogie Moran and Charlie Nelligan, not to mention the young Mikey Sheehy, would soon come on stream. Those successful U-21 sides in time produced the raw material for Kerry's evolving senior team. Shortly after Cork won the senior All-Ireland in 1973, Mikey graduated to the full Kerry senior team, playing that autumn in a National Football League match in Killarney.

'I was with the other subs at half-time, kicking the ball,' Mikey says. 'I went back in the dug out and the next thing somebody came over to me and said I was going in. I didn't have time to get nervous or overly excited. It was a wet day and Mick O'Dwyer was on the frees. He was kicking the frees for Kerry for years and he was having a bad day at the office. I was told I was to kick the frees when I went in and I said that was fine. Things went fairly OK for me and I kicked a few points from play. Then we got a free about 25 yards out in front of the goal and I kind of half went over to it but Micko wasn't going to let me kick it. Micko took it and, unfortunately, although I was sent in to kick the frees I didn't get to kick any that day. I wasn't going to be pushing my case. For a man who had been such a legend in the county, there was no way he was going to let this young fellow kick the frees on that particular day anyway.'

By 1975 the old order was gone from Kerry football and the new young stars were beginning to pour in. Slotting into the forwards that year were names like John Egan, Pat Spillane and Mikey Sheehy. Gone from the squad were fading stars like Mick O'Dwyer and Mick O'Connell. Mikey played throughout that year's championship campaign, scoring 0–4 against Cork in the Munster final and another 0–4 in the All-Ireland final. In the September decider against Dublin he also played his part in a crucial goal scored by John Egan, which helped secure the Sam Maguire Cup for the Kingdom.

'The goal that John Egan got resulted from a free that I should have scored from,' Mikey recalls. 'It was only about 40 yards out, although it was a wet kind of day. I sort of miss-hit it and one of the Dublin backs missed the ball and it broke to John. No better man, John put it in the back of the net and it kind of settled us down. It was a tremendous occasion and a fantastic atmosphere. I won't say we won comfortably but we got another goal in the second half and that was the start of a great run for us.'

The rise of Kerry in 1975 eventually culminated in the county's remarkable four All-Ireland triumphs in a row from 1978 to 1981, with two victories over Dublin and one each over Roscommon and Offaly. Throughout those championship campaigns Mikey Sheehy invariably struck devastating form. It wasn't uncommon for Mikey to chalk up personal tallies of 2–8, 2–5 and 3–5, as he did in various matches. He scored 2–6 against Dublin in the 1979 All-Ireland final and 1–6 against Roscommon in the following year's decider. Accompanied by players like Pat Spillane, Eoin Liston, John Egan, Ger Power and Ogie Moran, rare was the match in which Mikey Sheehy failed to register some combination of scores.

'It probably comes from practise and from confidence,' Mikey says of his scoring ability. 'You are only going to get a certain number of opportunities to score goals on big occasions and when the occasions arise you have to try to take them. In any big championship game I felt that if I got a chance I would hope to put it away. It's a confidence thing and sometimes it's from being in the right place at the right time. Maybe it's instinct but when you get your opportunity you just stick it away.

'Corner-forwards are the guys closest to the goal and they should be hovering. You're going to have to be moving around and switching sides and moving out the field maybe the odd occasion. But you're always supposed to be hovering in near the goal and when you get your opportunity you take it. In Killarney after training we would spend a lot of time practising one-on-ones with Charlie Nelligan. Micko would have us doing that. Even when he wouldn't be doing it, we'd be doing it ourselves, myself and Ger Power, John Egan, Eoin Liston, Pat Spillane, the whole lot of us. As Jack Nicklaus said years ago: "The more you practise, the luckier you get."

'I don't know if Páidí Ó Sé remembers this or not but when he was on our team he had an awful habit, before big games, of coming over to myself and John Egan and saying: "Take the points, the goals will come later on." He'd always feel that early in a game if we got a chance take the point because if a goalie made a save it would make a hero of him and raise his team. We often spoke about it and I would always have felt, and John I think as well, that if you got a chance in the first minute have a cut anyway because you mightn't get another chance.

'Our fitness and training helped too. I think we had four or five physical education teachers on the team but Micko very seldom looked for advice off them. He had his own formula for fitness and it certainly helped us down through the years. He nearly always had you fresh for a final. He was a great judge of a player's fitness. Certain years he might feel that some of us might need to put in an extra little bit of work coming up to the final. Other years he might say: "Look, you're in good shape, we'll just keep you ticking over." He was always a very good manager of players and of their condition. Most of the time he had us right for the finals in particular.'

Throughout the glory years from 1978 to 1981 there wasn't a single championship match in which Mikey Sheehy failed to score. In fact, he averaged almost eight points a game for those four years. There were many classic goals and points scored with style and deadly accuracy. As a free-taker, he couldn't be bettered. From play, he could score with relative ease. In terms of skill, there were few to match him in Kerry.

Unfortunately, lying in wait for Mikey Sheehy was the inevitable disappointment that faces players who operate at the cutting edge of the game. From Kerry's perspective, it couldn't have come at a worse time. The disaster occurred in the 1982 All-Ireland final at a time when Kerry were within sight of a historic five-in-a-row. Awarded a penalty, Mikey had the chance to put Kerry out of Offaly's reach. Instead, his penalty kick was dramatically saved by the Offaly goalkeeper Martin Furlong. It was the signal for an unlikely Offaly revival and the beginning of the end for Kerry's historic dream.

'I was very disappointed over that,' Mikey reflects. 'I didn't hit it well and I felt I wasn't playing well on the day. A lot of guys always say: "Maybe Jacko should have kicked it or John Egan should have kicked it or Eoin Liston should have kicked it." But it was funny that when the penalty was given there were no volunteers. I was thrown the ball. It was at a crucial stage in the game. Had that goal gone in, there's no doubt in my mind that we would have won the '82 final. But that's life. I wouldn't shirk it. If we had got another one and I had been asked to take it, I would have taken it too.

'Fair play to Offaly, they won an All-Ireland and they deserved to win it. Matt Connor kicked a few frees for them and they kept in contention. A lot of people said after the game that tactically we got it wrong or that Mick O'Dwyer got it wrong or that we went back in defence for the last 15 minutes to try and hold on to what we had. We were never told to do that. Whether we were all conscious that we wanted to make history or not, I don't know. Certainly we were never instructed to play a defensive game for the last 15 minutes or so. In most finals we'd finish very strong. We'd usually put teams away at that stage.

'Offaly kept plugging away and Séamus Darby got his goal. It was a tremendous goal, a great shot and history was not to be made by us winning number five. It was a bitter experience, I must say. It was one that took us a long time to get over. It even dragged on until the following year because in '83 we were beaten above in Cork. I'll be truthful with you, even in the dressing-room that day above in Páirc Uí Chaoimh the same disappointment wasn't there that was there in

'82. We still talk about it and we can still remember the bad points in the game, in particular the penalty miss.'

Throughout the mid-1980s Mikey Sheehy remained a central cog in Kerry's prolific scoring machine. He scored in every championship game he played in from 1984 to 1986, although his average dropped to 4.5 points a match. He produced goals against Galway in the 1984 All-Ireland semi-final and against Cork in Munster in 1985. There was a further goal against Tyrone in the All-Ireland final in 1986. Despite the departure of his partner John Egan at the end of 1984, little had changed in Kerry football. Sheehy, Spillane, Moran, Liston and Power still formed the core of attack and Kerry still dominated the All-Ireland championship.

In those years from 1984 to 1986 Mikey added a further three All-Ireland medals to his already impressive collection. Although he missed the 1984 All-Ireland final through injury, his haul of medals rose to the historic figure of eight, which remains an all-time record shared with his team-mates Pat Spillane, Páidí Ó Sé, Ogie Moran and Ger Power. Along the way, Kerry notched up victories over Dublin in 1984 and 1985 and over Tyrone in 1986. The Kingdom also extended their appearance record to an astonishing 10 All-Ireland finals in 12 years, which was nothing short of phenomenal.

'There's no doubt in my mind that had we won the 1982 All-Ireland final, we certainly wouldn't have won in '84, '85 and '86,' Mikey remarks. 'It was like an old car; we had a lot of mileage on the clock at that stage. I'll always remember 1983. I think it was either the Wednesday after or the Wednesday prior to the All-Ireland between Dublin and Galway when we started back in training. That was unheard-of in Kerry. Micko would always let us winter well and he'd bring us in maybe in February to shed a bit of weight off us if we were carrying a bit extra. But he got us earlier that year and pushed us right through the winter with the prime objective of winning back the All-Ireland the following year, which we did.

'I would always say that winning those three All-Irelands was a better achievement than winning a five-in-a-row. The first two games against Dublin were good battles but I felt that in the last one in '86 against Tyrone we were certainly lucky. Had they scored the penalty that Kevin McCabe blasted over the bar, I don't think there was any way back for us. They probably deserved to win an All-Ireland medal but when they got a goal there was nobody who could grasp it and say: "Look, we have these guys rattled." I think they were in shock that they were six or seven points ahead of us. They didn't realise that we were there for the taking. In the second half we kept plugging away and Pat Spillane got a great goal and I think we won well in the finish.

'It's always nice to say that you won a certain number of medals but you don't think about them. All you want to do is go out and win, to go out and perform to the best of your ability. There's nothing better than the winning feeling. I suppose the medals are there to decorate some corner of the house at some stage but I don't think any of our players have medals up to be viewed anywhere. The more you win the more you want to win, it's as simple as that, and the medal is just a bonus at the end of the day. It's there to say that you did it.'

It was said in Kerry that when Mikey Sheehy played at club level, crowd numbers swelled just to watch him. Without doubt his genius caught the public's imagination. It was clear to all those fortunate enough to see him play that they were in the presence of an extraordinary talent with a rare football intellect and a natural aptitude for the game. His scoring record alone was exceptional and his consistent marksmanship in major contests marked him out from his peers. As a free-taker, he knew no match. As a goal-poacher, he broke the hearts of great Cork and Dublin teams while thrilling packed venues in the process.

The twilight of Mikey's career also coincided with the end of Kerry's great years. In 1987, as captain, he led his county to a Munster final defeat by a resurgent Cork team. There would be no 'last hurrahs' for the Kerry team as they fell to three further successive defeats to their neighbours in Munster. As Kerry limped on, so too did Mikey Sheehy. Crippled by various injuries he struggled into 1988, when he was forced to retire from the game. By then he had accumulated a treasure chest of National Football League, Railway Cup, Munster Senior Football Championship and Kerry County Championship medals. He also had won seven All-Star awards. His subsequent selection on the Team of the Millennium marked the culmination of a remarkable career spanning eight senior All-Ireland medals and a coveted Footballer of the Year award won in 1979.

'I didn't really have the appetite in '87,' Mikey concludes. 'At that stage I had a few injuries and my left knee was giving me a lot of trouble. I had a lot of joint damage and I was struggling with my fitness. Shape-wise I wasn't too bad; I wasn't carrying much weight or anything like that. I had watched myself but I wasn't able to do two hard sessions in a row. My old knee would seize up and I was taking a few painkillers for it. I just felt that the hunger wasn't there.

'Around April of the same year I picked up an Achilles tendon injury on my good leg as a result of overcompensating. I struggled big-time during the year. We were beaten by Cork in a replay and we should have been beaten above in Páirc Uí Chaoimh. I played on at club football for a while but in 1988 I was playing a club game on Easter Sunday and I did my cruciate ligament in on my good knee. It was the only good bit of a leg I had left so that kind of made up my mind. I certainly wasn't going to play inter-county championship football that year. I would have liked to play club football for a few more years but that finished me. I had it operated on in 1990 just so that I could play a bit of golf and it's fine now.

'I look back on it with the feeling that I was very lucky to have come at an era when Kerry had a great manager and a great squad of players. I made great friends with those lads that I played with and also with players from other counties. If somebody had said to me when I was starting off my career that I was going to be lucky enough to play in ten finals and win eight, win a few All-Stars and see the world, I would have said: "God, if only that happens to me!" If you played in a couple of finals and won a couple of medals you'd be happy. So I look back on it with great pride.'

12. MATT CONNOR

IT WAS HARD TO IMAGINE A MORE UNEQUAL CONTEST. IN 1982 THE MIGHTY STARS FROM Kerry arrived at the All-Ireland final to tackle the rank outsiders from Offaly. The Kingdom were going for a historic five-in-a-row. The Faithful County faced two All-Ireland final defeats in succession. Arguably the finest team in Gaelic football history togged out in the Kerry colours. Lined up against them was a team consisting, in the main, of a collection of brothers from an unfashionable county with a modest football legacy of just two All-Ireland senior titles.

That day in September 1982 Offaly's deadly sharpshooter Matt Connor travelled to Croke Park with his brother Richie, the Offaly captain. Their first cousins, Liam and Tomás O'Connor, were also on the team. Not to be outdone, the Darby and Fitzgerald families provided a set of brothers each. Just to round it off, the Lowry family committed three brothers to the Offaly cause. Reflecting the size of the county and the concentrated nature of their football activities, it was almost inevitable that Offaly's charge for the championship title would be a family affair.

Out of those five families it was the young Matt Connor who pulled his team back into contention with two crucial points in the latter stages of the game. Suddenly, Offaly were on a roll and Kerry were rattled. Although still leading by two points, Kerry lost the plot and conceded a famous goal to Séamus Darby. For the men from the Faithful County, revenge was sweet. On the back of All-Ireland semi-final and All-Ireland final defeats by Kerry in 1980 and 1981 respectively, Offaly had struck gold, securing the Sam Maguire Cup for just the third time in the county's history.

'There were five sets of brothers on the team,' Matt recalls. 'It was a big family thing and I suppose it helps that part of your family is involved. It takes the pressure off. You're spreading the pressure around the family. We weren't given much of a chance by anybody except ourselves. We believed that we could do it. We had played them twice and they had beaten us every time but we were getting closer to them. We knew we had to play well and keep with them and hopefully we'd get the break near the end. It was going to be a hard battle and we knew that we were going to have to have a bit of luck.

'The build-up suited us very well because Kerry were going for the famous five-in-a-row and all the pressure was on them. No one gave us a chance. That's always a great way to go into a final. It was up to them what they were doing. We kept away from that. We only worried about our own game. Eugene McGee kept us as underdogs and that's the way we faced into it. There was a lot of talk around that time of the five-in-a-row but we didn't concentrate on that. Games won't be won by talking about T-shirts with "Five-in-a-Row" on them and trying to build yourself up in that way. You have to work on your own game and you have to work on the weaknesses of the other team and the strengths of your own team.

'They were probably the best football team ever. They had a lethal forward line, an extremely good back line and a great midfield. They really had no weaknesses. We had to work hard on the day and give a good team effort and have a good team spirit, keep ahead and never give up. One very important thing was that Eugene McGee put my brother Richie in at centre-forward. That was a key decision on that day because the year before Tim Kennelly had absolutely cleaned up. He was going to make sure that the main reason we were beaten in 1981 wasn't going to happen again. He put him as a kind of stopper and a playmaker at centre-forward and that worked a treat. Another thing was that Eoin Liston was the key man in the Kerry forward line and we had to stop him and stop the supply of ball to him. Liam O'Connor did quite a good job in that sense on the day and the players out the field did a lot of hard work and hard grafting to stop the ball going into the Kerry full-forward line.

'The first half was open and it was a very good game of football. The second half it started raining fairly heavily and the game deteriorated a good bit. I think Kerry dominated for a long time and we were lucky enough to stay with them. Martin Furlong's penalty save was very important. If they had scored that, I don't think we would have come back. The rest is history. We were four points behind and we got two frees and it put us two points behind. Then a long ball came to Séamus Darby and he banged it in the net. It was a super shot. All Croke Park went wild but there was still a minute and a half left in the game and we had to hold on with all our might. We had to live on our nerves just to hold on. Everyone was hoping that we could do it. Then the final whistle went and we had it won.

'It was super when it was all over. We had done it because we had put in a lot of work over five or six years. It's wonderful to achieve your goal after all those years. It takes a while and it doesn't sink in straight away. It's hard to believe it. There was great euphoria after the game and it was super in the dressing-room. There was great excitement. Because the supporters and other people around are so excited, you get caught up in it. But it takes a while for it to sink in with the players and to realise that you have won it.

'The homecoming was wonderful in Tullamore. I remember the homecoming in 1971, when Willie Bryan brought the cup to Offaly. The town was unbelievably full. It was a wonderful night and it was the first time the Sam Maguire Cup came to Offaly. I was very young at the time and my father and mother brought me into the town. I'll always remember it as a great night. I suppose our night was like that, although you don't remember it the same because you are involved. For the people looking at it, it's more special.'

Coming from Walsh Island in Offaly, Matt Connor was destined to achieve football success. With a father who was a top-class player with the local Walsh Island club, football was clearly in the genes. Matt's uncles also played football. Offaly legend Willie Bryan was his first cousin. Matt's brother Murt helped spearhead Offaly's rise to football prominence in the 1970s, winning All-Ireland medals in the county's first two senior championship successes in 1971 and 1972. In time, both Matt and his brother Richie progressed to the Walsh Island and Offaly teams, where they were accompanied by their first cousins Liam and Tomás O'Connor. To add to the picture, brother Richie was captain of the victorious 1982 championship side while Matt was the star forward who cracked home goals and points.

'There was nothing but football in our family,' Matt remarks. 'Every Sunday, every chance we got, we were out playing football in our local field. My brother Murt won two All-Irelands in 1971 and 1972. I looked up to all that team, especially Tony McTague and Willie Bryan. When Murt was involved, I would meet them at games and they would come and collect Murt at times. I'd be looking at them and I would be inspired by all of them. You wouldn't get to know the players but you'd get to see them and be closer to them than most fellows. It was great to have my brother involved. Watching them making a breakthrough and winning the All-Ireland in 1971 was a great thrill and a great memory for me. They were my heroes at the time.

'We were steeped in football. There were four of us from Walsh Island on the Offaly team. There was Liam O'Connor and also Tomás O'Connor, who were brothers and first cousins of ours, together with Richie and myself. We only lived a mile apart and we played football together for all our youth. We travelled everywhere and we were always together. From one Sunday to the next we were playing with Walsh Island or Offaly, and for six or seven years we were in one carload to games all around the country. We played with Leinster together as well. It was Walsh Island, Offaly or Leinster every Sunday playing together.'

The revival of Offaly in the late 1970s was inspired by the appointment of a remarkable new manager by the name of Eugene McGee. A marvellous strategist with a visionary view of the game, he had already steered University College, Dublin to unprecedented All-Ireland club success. Now, following his take-over of Offaly, he set about blending a new football side from the best of the old and the most promising of the new. Combining remnants of the victorious team of the early 1970s with an infusion of new blood, McGee's aim was to mould a team capable of challenging for Leinster and All-Ireland honours.

'When Eugene McGee arrived he had to build a new team,' Matt says. 'He got a lot of new players. Four or five of them were from the 1976 minor team that was beaten in the Leinster minor final by Dublin. There were also four or five players that won All-Irelands in 1971 and '72. He had to blend them all together. He brought great organisation to the county. He had new ideas about total football and different ideas that were very new to the game, especially in Offaly. He had us going away on weekends. We even went away to Spain to train. I think we were the first team to do that and it was totally Eugene McGee's idea. He got the winning belief into us and I think we went a step further every year from when he took over.

'We played Dublin in 1978 in the Leinster semi-final and we lost. We very nearly beat Dublin in 1979 in the Leinster final and it was a very disappointing result for us. We had got closer both years. We came back in 1980 to beat them. It was a huge thing at the time to beat Dublin because they were a super team in Leinster. We seemed to be improving all the time and we were going one step further every year. When we won the Leinster final in 1980 that was a big breakthrough because Offaly hadn't won a Leinster since '73. That was seven years of a break.'

The re-emergence of Offaly in 1980 from the football wilderness was accompanied by the arrival of a new football star in the shape of Matt Connor. In the Leinster final against Dublin, Matt demonstrated his football skills with a dramatic goal that effectively settled the match. Later, he scored a remarkable 2–9 against Kerry in the All-Ireland semi-final. Whether playing off his left or right, or whether scoring from play or from frees, Matt brought a devastating potency and power to the Offaly attack. Unfortunately, Matt's extraordinary 2–9 in the championship semi-final, scored against arguably the finest team in football history, wasn't enough to secure an Offaly victory. His team succumbed to Kerry by 4–15 to 4–10.

'Kerry beat us well enough in the end,' Matt concedes. 'It was kind of a free-flowing game and it was one of those games where the scores come a bit easier. Some days you have that, where the goals go in. Kerry were very positive in their attitude and I think at that stage they were playing very good football. They were a very good attacking team and I suppose they left a few openings at the back because of that.

'I was becoming the main scorer on the team at that stage. I had been the free-taker for some time but, at that stage, things were being set up for me as well. Eugene McGee was getting them to set the ball up for me for scoring. I was lucky to have got involved in a good forward line and the midfielders were very good distributors of the ball to me. I probably was the main scorer that year. On a given day you would get a couple of goals and along with frees the score can mount up. Sometimes you have good days and other days they just don't go in.

'I was always a forward from my youth. I loved scoring and especially scoring goals. It was always a great thrill and I always wanted to be the top scorer in every game I played. In every team I played with, I was probably the free-taker. I did a lot of practise with frees and always had a ball in my hand. I was practising scoring all the time. When I went out to practise I always practised to the goals and very little else. I was always shooting at the goals or taking frees. That's the practise I liked. Where other people might do a lot of training in other ways, I'd always prefer to be doing target-practise.

'When Eugene McGee came in, he had me as a free-taker. I think the second or third year I became the free-taker. We practised frees nearly every night in training. We practised shooting and did a lot of practising on forward playing. Our midfield weren't really encouraged to do much scoring, more so setting up balls, which was very good for forwards. Brendan Lowry and myself were probably the two main score-getters. Our game was built on the idea that we would be doing most of the scoring.'

In 1981 Offaly inched closer to achieving their All-Ireland ambitions with another Leinster final success, this time with a victory over Laois. That September Eugene McGee's men faced Kerry for the second year in succession, on this occasion in the championship decider. By now the rivalry between Offaly and Kerry was replacing the Dublin–Kerry rivalry of the previous decade. Unfortunately, Kerry were set on winning their fourth All-Ireland in succession while Offaly's dreams of emulating the success of the early 1970s were to prove premature. In the 1981 All-Ireland final, Kerry beat Offaly by 1–12 to 0–8.

'We were getting one step closer,' Matt says. 'It took us three attempts to beat Dublin in Leinster and it would eventually take us three attempts to beat Kerry. But we were playing two of the greatest teams ever. Probably Kerry were the greatest team ever and Dublin could be put down as one of the greatest as well, perhaps even the second-best team. At the time it was hard to make the breakthrough with those two teams, first to beat Dublin and get out of Leinster and then to play Kerry, who were a great team.'

Offaly's remarkable run continued in 1982 with their historic victory over Kerry in the All-Ireland final. McGee's team had finally tasted triumph over Kerry while simultaneously shattering the Kingdom's aspirations of winning five-in-a-row All-Irelands. It was a remarkable run of success for an Offaly team that had now replaced Dublin as the leading force in Leinster. Their 1982 Leinster final victory over Dublin secured their third Leinster title in a row. Their 1982 All-Ireland success marked their third successive appearance in the penultimate or ultimate stages of the championship. Above all, along the way they had conquered the two great teams of the era, Dublin and Kerry.

As the championship began in 1983, there was no reason to believe that Offaly's run of success would come to an end. The team was playing attractive football. Players like Matt Connor were on the top of their form. Yet, despite playing well, Offaly were beaten by Dublin in the 1983 Leinster final and it would be Dublin, not Offaly, who would win the next three Leinster titles in succession. For Offaly, the year 1983 marked the end and not the beginning of a new football era.

'We were going very well in '83 and we were probably playing our best football ever in Leinster,' Matt says. 'Dublin caught us in the Leinster final. They played super that day and we just lost it. Once we lost it, we never got it back. But we definitely had a good chance in 1983 of winning the All-Ireland again and probably should have only that we got caught by Dublin. Maybe we were a bit overconfident because we'd beaten Dublin handy enough the year before. We just got caught anyway. But it was a superb Dublin performance that day, I certainly can remember that.'

On Christmas Day 1984 the football world was shocked by the news of a tragic car accident in County Offaly. As news filtered through, it became clear that the smash involved an Offaly footballer by the name of Matt Connor. Having survived the crash, Matt eventually underwent six months of rehabilitation in Dublin. Unfortunately, in time it became clear that this great Offaly star would be confined to a wheelchair and that he would never play football again. As a result of that tragic event, Matt was left paraplegic, Offaly lost their star forward and Gaelic football lost one of its finest exponents. At the age of 25 his career had come to a tragic and premature end.

'I was going home from Tullamore on Christmas Day in 1984 to my Christmas dinner,' Matt recalls. 'My car went out of control and I was thrown out of the car and landed on my back. I hurt my back, damaged my spine and I suffered paraplegia from that accident. That finished my football career in 1984. When I had the accident I suppose football wasn't the main priority at that stage. It was just a complete change of life in that I was not able to walk again. It was a case of going from playing football with Offaly to trying to do the simple things in life again.

'There were a lot more important things and football wasn't a priority at that stage. For the next six months I was ready to adapt and get on with my life and try to live a new life with my injury. But later on, in a year's time or so, I probably began to miss football more. I had adapted to a new life and then I saw a few more things that brought me back a bit. I probably missed football more then. I suppose at some stage you're going to have to finish playing anyway but it was just a bit sooner than I expected.'

In many ways, both the career of Matt Connor and the Offaly revival of the early 1980s came to a simultaneous end. Following Matt's departure, Offaly dropped back into the football wilderness, where once again they played second fiddle to both Meath and Dublin in the Leinster championship. That was hardly surprising given Matt's record as Offaly's leading marksman throughout the county's resurgence, not to mention his feats in scoring the likes of 2–9 in his county's famous 1980 battle with Kerry. His consistent performances secured him three All-Star awards, three successive Leinster titles and a single All-Ireland while marking him out as one of the finest forwards in the history of Gaelic football.

'It was a good era,' Matt concludes. 'Any time you win a Leinster championship in a county like Offaly, it's a good era. We won three Leinster titles and an All-Ireland. I enjoyed my time playing during that era. We were playing probably two of the greatest teams ever, Kerry and Dublin. We played in a lot of packed stadiums. When you're playing in the summer sun in July in a Leinster final or All-Ireland semi-final, they are good times.

'The years 1980, '81 and '82 were great years for Offaly. We won a hurling All-Ireland in 1981 and a football All-Ireland in 1982. We won two Leinsters in 1981 and we were in two All-Ireland finals that year also. Offaly is a very small county and we'll have bad times and good times. Those were very good years for us and we achieved a lot. It's all about achieving things when you have fairly good teams. I think those teams achieved to the best of their ability. We put a lot of work into it. We spent five years getting one step further every year and we eventually won. It was a great achievement for a county like Offaly.'

13. PAT SPILLANE

PUMPING WEIGHTS ON A COLD, DAMP GARAGE FLOOR WHILE SURROUNDED BY RATS
and mice is far from the glamour side of a footballer's existence. You
lie on your stomach and back, your body ice-cold from the draughts.
Blasts of air sweep in through the cracks in the building. Dark winter
clouds overshadow the sky outside. Rats and mice scurry across the
floor, their movement accompanying the sound of your breathing.
Your mind fights boredom. Every nerve in your body tells you to
quit.

In a garage in County Kerry in the winter months of early 1983,
such was the scene of Pat Spillane's recovery from a near-
catastrophic, career-threatening injury. With a ruptured anterior
cruciate ligament in his left knee and recovering from remedial
surgery, he took to the garage adjoining the family pub to resurrect
his career. Day after day he lay prostrate on the floor restoring the
power in his legs. Driven by relentless determination and a superhuman will to succeed, he battled to revive a career that only months
before had appeared to be finished.

A winner by then of five All-Ireland senior medals, Pat Spillane
had tragically damaged his knee in a club match. Known for his
high-powered, twisting, darting runs, undoubtedly his knee was
already ravaged from the wear and tear of his football exertions.
Now, however, the cruciate ligament had finally snapped and the
prospects for the future were grim. On the Kerry front, the team had
just relinquished the chance of a historic five-in-a-row by losing the
1982 All-Ireland final, with a crippled Pat Spillane playing as sub.
On a personal level, after winning more accolades and awards than
most footballers could ever dream of, including Footballer of the
Year, it appeared that Pat Spillane's career might well be over.

'Looking back on it now, it was horrendous,' Pat recalls. 'I bought a weight machine and installed it inside in the garage. On several occasions either mice or rats used to be in the garage. I could see them particularly when I'd be doing hamstring exercises where you lie on your stomach. I'd say: "Oh God, he's gone behind me." I'd jump a mile if I saw a mouse or a rat but I just was so single-minded and so focused that I kept doing it. I just said: "I'm going to keep at it." And I did.

'I drove myself to an extreme. I did weights three days a week. If the second or the third day of training corresponded with Christmas Day or New Year's Eve or New Year's Day, I trained. I never missed a single training session even though doing weights on your own is very difficult because you alone are doing the driving. There's no one else. It was something from within. Having won five All-Ireland medals and having achieved every accolade that could have been achieved, why should I want to go through it all again? I'd wonder every now and again if there was going to be any success out of it. I just went through it to build up my leg and to get fit again.

'I came back a very driven man because I was told by quite eminent orthopaedic surgeons in this country that I'd never again play football. When you rupture a cruciate ligament it's the same as tearing an elastic band. No matter what way you put it back together again it's never going to be as strong as it was prior to the injury. I had to educate myself to do things with my right knee which I used always do with my left. I always jumped off my left foot, now I had to jump off my right. I used to step and swerve off my left foot, now I had to educate myself to do everything on the right. I had to be cute. I couldn't go in for 50-50 balls. I couldn't leave the left foot exposed because if it got hit it would have buckled. It was about 60 to 70 per cent what it had been prior to the injury.'

Few players brought more colour and flamboyance to Gaelic football than Pat Spillane from Templenoe, County Kerry. From his first appearances as a footballer he oozed style and confidence. By the age of 18 he had already graduated to the Kerry senior team, making his first appearance in March 1974. That league contest with Galway saw Pat listed as eleventh substitute. Brought on that day, he scored his first points for his county. A National Football League winner in '74, he retained his place as sub for Kerry's unsuccessful championship campaign, which culminated in defeat by Cork in the Munster final. Mick O'Connell was sub for Kerry that day. Sitting in the dug out alongside the 37-year-old O'Connell was the 18-year-old Pat Spillane.

'I remember sitting on the subs' bench in Killarney with Pat Griffin and Mick O'Connell on either side of me,' Pat recollects. 'I always remember Mick O'Connell was being brought on as a sub late in the second half. The game was out of Kerry's reach and Cork were coasting and Mick said to the Kerry County Secretary: "Put a youngster on, there's no future bringing the likes of me on." He was very fair because most old fellows would jump at the chance to prove selectors wrong and prove that they were still capable of doing something.

'He reluctantly went on and I remember a Cork player embarrassed Mick when he soloed out in front of him. It wasn't a good thing to do; you hate to see a guy who was one of the greatest footballers of all time being humiliated. But '74 was the start and it was nice to be involved. I played league in '74. I didn't play championship in '74 but it gave me the taste of championship football and it gave me the taste of Munster finals. When you get beaten in a Munster final by Cork it really makes you feel all the more determined to come back and try to finish off the job and go one better the following year.'

In 1975, with an average age of 22, a new-look, youthful Kerry side embarked on the search for All-Ireland glory. Boosted by a Pat Spillane goal, they cruised past Cork in the Munster final. Inspired by another Spillane goal, they crushed Sligo in the semi-final. In the minor All-Ireland final Pat's brother, Mike Spillane, collected a valued minor medal. A short while later, big brother Pat was sharing in Kerry's senior success over Dublin and winning his first all-Ireland senior medal. With Kenmare's Mickey O'Sullivan injured and en route to hospital, it was left to his team-mate, Pat Spillane, to collect the cup. Aged 19, Pat had arrived in big-time Gaelic football.

'It was a dream only that it was reality,' Pat says. 'It was like Goran Ivanisevic's quote after Wimbledon: "I hope I don't wake up and discover that it was all a dream." The enormity of it and the achievement of it only struck me in recent times. One of the greatest accolades in Gaelic football is to receive the All-Ireland trophy in

Croke Park on All-Ireland final day. And that I did.

'I was young, very immature and it was something that I just took for granted at the time. Looking back on it now, it's a fabulous achievement. I don't think even my children realise it at this stage because there are no photographs around the house. I don't think I ever got a photograph of me receiving the cup and I don't think I ever saw a video of that '75 final again. It was a fabulous start to a career. After that, for all of us there was only one way to go and that was down, which we did.

'We were a bunch of youngsters, 18 known bachelors, fun-loving guys. We had a great time. We had cruised through '75, won an All-Ireland medal, got our holiday, got the accolades, got the pats on the back, went to functions. It was a roller-coaster ride. In '76 I think we believed that it was our right to go through. It had gone to our heads and it was just our right to go through and win another All-Ireland.

'We got a little bit of a fright in Munster but then we got through to the All-Ireland final and we said: "Ah, it's Dublin again." Certainly the same effort wasn't there. The Rose of Tralee festival was on a couple of weeks before the All-Ireland, the players were now stars or superstars and they were invited to the functions. Everyone can share responsibility. Perhaps physically we were right but mentally we certainly weren't right. We got what we deserved and we were beaten by Dublin in '76.

'The '77 semi-final against Dublin was considered to be the greatest football match of all time. I always beg to differ. Funny enough, any game that Kerry won doesn't rank at all in terms of being a great match. I can never understand that. Anyway, in '77 the first half was quite riddled with errors and there were a lot of misplaced passes. If I were analysing it on television I'd be criticising a lot of aspects of it. But it was played at a tremendous pace and there was ferocity in the game. I would point to a turning point in '77, where there was a line-ball that should have been given to Kerry and it went to Dublin and a goal came out of it immediately. A game can turn on little things like that. Looking back on it now, we certainly didn't deserve to win; the better team won on the day.'

There can be no doubting Pat Spillane's contribution to Kerry's four-in-a-row from 1978 to 1981. A prolific sharpshooter, Pat rifled home goals and points while destroying opposing defences and bamboozling his markers. He chalked up huge scoring tallies in Kerry's championship campaigns, becoming something of a scourge to Cork in Munster while also claiming the limelight in All-Ireland semi-finals and finals. He delivered the first of his three All-Ireland final Man of the Match performances in 1978. He was voted Footballer of the Year for 1978. He also added All-Star awards and Railway Cup successes to his five All-Ireland medals won up to 1981. Still only in his mid-20s, his rise was meteoric.

'I had learned from '77,' Pat reflects. 'I think I had developed a sort of selfish style and I was inclined to over-hold the ball and over-carry the ball. I had been dropped in '77 for the first league match. I was very annoyed and said they were wrong. The first temptation was to sulk and refuse to turn up as sub in our next match. But I always looked on the positive side and I always believed in trying to prove people wrong. I've always been trying to do it throughout my football career. I would have been slow to admit to being selfish but the message got through to me from O'Dwyer and I think I became more of a team player. It certainly helped in '78 and onwards.

'In those years, particularly '78 and '79, we genuinely knew in our heart and soul that no one was going to beat us. They didn't either; they didn't come within a million miles of it. We were moulding into a complete unit at that stage, into what was the greatest football team of all time. We couldn't see ourselves being beaten and we weren't beaten. We were really a team. Perhaps in other counties star players can become prima donnas but not so in Kerry. Any one of the six forwards on their day could have been the match-winner or we could have had a different match-winner. We were never dependent on a Pat Spillane or Jack O'Shea or Eoin Liston to produce the goods. The other five or the other fourteen could produce the goods.

'We came from different parts of the county and we wouldn't have met socially, but when it came to training or when it came to games we were part of a unit. When we did a deal, whether it was for jerseys or boots or holidays or whatever, every one of the 30 got their share. There was no one person that was allowed to become greater than the team. I think that was very important in our subsequent successes. We went down together as a team and we shared our success as a team. That was the strongest point in O'Dwyer's management. An individual might have got the accolades in the media but amongst us players we were all one.'

The All-Ireland finals of 1981 and 1982 were memorable for Pat Spillane for very mixed reasons indeed. If truth were told, his career should never have extended beyond August 1981, when he damaged his knee playing for Templenoe in a club match in Kenmare. With his knee blown up like a balloon, he tried physiotherapy, heat therapy and old-fashioned rest. Although effectively crippled with an unstable knee, Pat was selected as sub for the 1981 All-Ireland final against Offaly. Brought on with just minutes to go, he won what was then his fifth All-Ireland medal on the field of play.

Throughout 1982 Pat Spillane sporadically played for the Kerry senior team. The knee problem continued to flare up, with the knee every so often collapsing beneath him and swelling like a balloon. Diagnosed as a snapped cruciate ligament, the medical advice was bleak. Almost no one in sport at that time had revived a career after such an abominable injury. Spurred on by Kerry's march to a historic five-in-a-row, Pat kept going. It wasn't until after Kerry's dream came unstuck against Offaly in the All-Ireland final that he faced long-overdue surgery in Cambridge. The operation was scheduled for November 1982.

'The selectors gave me every chance to recover in 1981,' Pat recalls. 'They did a fitness test on the Saturday night and I knew in my heart and soul that the leg wasn't up to it. The Kerry team doctor and Mick O'Dwyer were at the fitness session and they were quite happy with me. I didn't decide until the Sunday morning. It would have been very easy to be selfish and say: "I'm going to play in an All-Ireland final and I can come off." After all, to start an All-Ireland final is all-important. But by playing I would be leaving my colleagues down. The one thing I've learned is that there's no point in telling people that you've played a bad game because you've carried an injury or because you were sick or you had the flu or something like that. If you're not 100 per cent fit for a match you just don't make yourself available. I didn't make myself available.

'I can remember the All-Ireland final of '81 for two particular incidents. One was that the lads wouldn't allow the team photograph to be taken unless I stood in with them. I was sitting in the dug out having declared myself unfit to play but I can recall the tremendous reception I got running across the field to get the photograph taken.

I think it's a memory that will always linger in my mind. It was a very nice touch by the lads and it's something that I shall never forget. The second thing, which is even a nicer touch, is that when Kerry had pulled clear with three or four minutes to go, the Kerry selectors brought me on although they knew in their heart and soul that I was dragging a leg behind. It has meant that I won all my eight All-Ireland medals on the field of play. That's a nice achievement. It was also nice to know that I had played in all of the four-in-a-row.

'In '82 I played part of the All-Ireland final. I came on at half-time and I wasn't fit at all. I shouldn't have been there because of the knee. I had my cruciate ligament problem since 1981 but I hung on for 12 months building up and strengthening my legs just to hang in there and see if I could be part of that five-in-a-row. Looking at it now, I should have just pulled out in '81, had the operation and hoped to be back for '82. While I got a point, it was only a quarter of Pat Spillane that was out on the field, not the real Pat Spillane and not the Pat Spillane that was capable of giving 100 per cent to Kerry football.'

Although he missed 1983 while recovering from his injury, a reinvigorated Pat Spillane returned to the Kerry team for the 1984 season. Having first of all shared in Kerry's success in the National Football League, he then proceeded to score a brace of goals against Cork in the Munster final. As if he had never departed the scene, Pat then produced a Man of the Match performance in the 1984 All-Ireland final against Dublin. After adding another championship medal to his collection in 1985, he repeated his Man of the Match performance in the 1986 final against Tyrone. That day Pat scored the finest goal of his career while delivering his greatest performance in a Kerry shirt. He also won his record eighth All-Ireland medal while becoming Footballer of the Year for 1986.

'There are three All-Irelands that stand out for me,' Pat says. 'There was '75 because it was my first, a brilliant occasion. There was '84 because, having been told that I'd never play football again, I found myself back in Croke Park. I had a fabulous match. It was one of those days that everything went right and I scored probably the best points that I ever scored in Croke Park. There was one from under the Nally Stand and another from the Cusack Stand side. It was, I think, my second-best performance in an All-Ireland final. To come back and play, get Man of the Match and win an All-Ireland after believing that your football career was over was great.

'I'll also always remember '86 because that was my finest performance in an All-Ireland final. There are days when you go out and everything you try the ball goes the other way. In the '86 final against Tyrone, no matter where I ran the ball was there, no matter what I did it came off. You have days like that. I suppose some players make their own luck but certainly luck was on our side. I would be very much of the belief that Tyrone should have beaten us. They were six points up, got a penalty just after half-time and missed the penalty, which went over the bar. Instead of having a nine-point lead they had only a seven-point lead. That gave us a chink of hope.

'We kept ploughing on and I scored my best score ever. I palmed it against Tyrone that year. It was one of those things, I never did it before and I never have done it since. It's one of those things that sports people do and you question after: "Why did I do it?" It's something I can't answer. You suddenly do something that you've never, ever done in training and you've never done in a game before, where you dive full-length and you palm the ball in the opposite direction. If it doesn't come off, you'd look the greatest idiot in the whole world. Luckily for me it did come off. It was my finest hour in Croke Park and I got Man of the Match.

'I was 31 years of age and we weren't a great team. The team of '86 was really a pale shadow of the Kerry teams that had won All-Irelands previously. I suppose we should have seen the writing on the wall that we were starting to move downhill and maybe we should have got out while we were at the top. I suppose being the greedy whores that we were we kept going. But '86 was a lovely year, a fabulous year and I'll always remember it with great pleasure.'

Mick O'Dwyer left the Kerry set-up in 1989 just two years ahead of Pat Spillane. After playing top-level football for the best part of two decades, Pat finally hung up his inter-county boots in 1991. Like many of the great players he played with, Pat left behind memories of stylish, fluent football combined with the sort of individual talent and enormous skill that may never again be seen in the game. In Pat's case, the fruits of success were to be seen in the eight senior All-Ireland medals, twelve Munster titles, nine All-Star awards, four National Football Leagues and four Railway Cups that he won.

By the time he retired, the golden age of Kerry football had come to a close. The era of Kerry dominance had ended and most of the great players of the 1970s and '80s had left the game. Without doubt, the final years were a pale reflection of the successful years that went before. On the playing front, there were four successive Munster final defeats by Cork. On a personal level, some vitriolic abuse and criticism were voiced by less-than-happy fans in County Kerry. It was an unfortunate and less-than-deserving end to the career of one of the finest footballers ever to grace the game.

'I had eight All-Ireland medals and I was playing and soldiering on with Kerry and getting ridiculed,' Pat says of his final days. 'I remember I got particular criticism one time at a county championship game from supporters and it really hurt me. It was cruel stuff that they threw and it made me realise how fickle Kerry supporters are. I mean, past glories count for nothing. You're only as good as your last game.

'I think those years made me a much harder person and they made me become totally immune to criticism. Now I don't give a tuppenny. I did in those years and I found it very hard. Eventually, it just taught me to be harder and now criticism to me is like water off a duck's back. It doesn't bother me at all. The way I look at it is that I do what I want to do because I want to do it myself.

'Once you're retired the phone doesn't start hopping with hundreds and hundreds of people thanking you for your contribution to Kerry football. When you're gone, you're gone and that's it. I know in my heart and soul that if somebody had said they needed me back for another year I'd be stupid enough and naïve enough to probably say: "I'll give it one more crack for you." But no one ever asked me back and thankfully they didn't.

'The way I look at it now is not with bitterness or anything like that. I had an absolutely fabulous time with Kerry and in my Gaelic football career. It's only in recent years that I've realised the enormity of what we did achieve and the joy and success that we had and that we brought to so many people. I am very proud having been part of the greatest football team of all time. It's something that I'll take to my grave and it's a fabulous legacy to have been part of what was probably one of the greatest sporting teams of all codes.'

14. JACK O'SHEA

CHOOSING YOUR FOOTBALL IDOLS IN KERRY HAS ALWAYS BEEN A DIFFICULT TASK. QUITE literally, there's a pantheon of stars to pick from. It all depends on when you were born and what part of the county you come from. From the distant past there's Paddy Bawn Brosnan and Tadhgie Lyne. From recent times there's Séamus Moynihan and Maurice Fitzgerald. There are even four-in-a-row and three-in-a-row teams to revere. In fact, there isn't a decade without someone to look up to. However, if you grew up in the 1960s two legends stood out above all the rest. Their names were Mick O'Connell and Mick O'Dwyer.

For Jack O'Shea, who in time would become Footballer of the Year on four occasions, there was a bonus to growing up in Cahirciveen. O'Connell and O'Dwyer frequently came there to practise their skills. Away from the Kerry squad they toiled hour after hour, fine-tuning their high-fielding, shooting and kicking. They worked with relentless determination, at one with each other as they sharpened their game. Watching them was a future Kerry midfielder who would eventually win seven All-Ireland senior medals while reproducing the skills he observed in Cahirciveen. In time, many would say that in finesse and technique it was O'Shea who carried the style of O'Dwyer and O'Connell into the 1970s and '80s.

'They were an inspiration to me,' Jack O'Shea says. 'They came to the local field, which was right opposite my house in Cahirciveen, and I used to act as their ball boy. They trained and practised and I saw the two of them doing all sorts of things with the football. They were standing four and five yards apart, hammering the ball at one another, trying to catch the ball away from their bodies with their hands. They spent a huge amount of time shooting, kicking the ball from 40 and 50 yards apart, up in the air fielding, all the different aspects of the game. I think I learned so much from them at an early age.

'At evening time when I would come home from school, if I didn't go to the football field I went down to the gables of local houses and I had the ball and was kicking it up against the wall. I was imagining I was Mick O'Connell jumping up for the ball or Mick O'Dwyer shooting for a score. But I think the thing that stood to me most from watching them was the amount of time that they put in. I don't think the other Kerry players on the team would have been putting in the same amount of work. They trained on the days they weren't training with Kerry. I think at that time, in the 1960s, they trained twice a week with the Kerry team but the other three or four days of the week they met up and they put in all that effort. I don't think I could have had two better people to prepare me for my career ahead.'

If only because of the culture he grew up in, Jack O'Shea seemed destined to achieve football success. Coming from South Kerry, there was a special affinity with the art of playing with a round ball. In the 1960s South Kerry boasted both Mick O'Connell and Mick O'Dwyer and that alone was an incentive for any aspiring footballer from the area. The era he arrived in also was a bonus. In 1975, with Jacko at full-forward, the Kerry minors won the All-Ireland title. With the seniors making it a double triumph that year, the county was flushed with success.

To anyone watching the minors at Croke Park in 1975, it was clear that a new talent had arrived in Kerry football. Observers of club football were far from surprised. Already, Jacko was turning in impressive midfield performances at club minor level. He had previously shown promise as full-back and in the half-back line. In fact, such was his strength, talent and style that he was playing all over the field. Whether he was performing for his school, his club or for the minors of Kerry, Jack O'Shea clearly was one for the future.

'At primary level and through my primary years, I actually played as a back,' Jacko reflects. 'The first final I played at primary level I played at full-back. Then I went out and played at the half-back line in subsequent years. I was a versatile type of player and I think I was pretty good at the old football. I was used to different positions, so I got great variety in my game. I spent a lot of time at skills and kicking and practising and that sort of stuff, so no matter what position I played in I was happy to play in it.

'I happened to end up at midfield basically through my stamina and my strength. I did a lot of running when I was young. Going to school in Cahirciveen we did a lot of cross-country running. Another thing that stood to me as well was that my father was a great beagle hunter in Kerry, which entails a lot of mountain climbing. From a very young age I spent most of my Sunday afternoons on the mountains, hunting with the beagles. I got great strength in my legs and my muscles and my upper body from running up and down mountains and jumping ditches and jumping over fences and that sort of stuff. I think that stood to me as the years went by.

'I first made the Kerry minor team in 1974. To my surprise I was dropped for the Munster final, so that was a big disappointment for me. The following year I got on to the Kerry minor team at full-forward. Playing minor at club level at that time, I was playing midfield all the time. I was probably one of the most prominent midfielders at minor level. I don't know what put it into their heads to put me in at full-forward. But I enjoyed it because when you're that young and you play in the forwards you're putting your name on the scoreboard. It was a great year for me at minor level. I was contributing quite a lot and I was getting my name on the scoreboard and that's what kept me going and kept me happy. They were using me as a target-man a lot and I enjoyed my football in there. But I was a natural midfielder all that time.'

As a result of his exploits at minor level, Jack O'Shea soon caught the eye of the Kerry U-21 and senior selectors. Elevated to the Kerry U-21 side, Jack would shortly pick up three U-21 All-Ireland medals with this enormously talented team. Players from the successful minor and U-21 sides soon blended into the senior squad. Names like Mikey Sheehy, Ogie Moran and Pat Spillane worked their way on to the senior panel. Another player to arrive was midfielder Seán Walsh. Soon, Seán Walsh and Jack O'Shea would form a deadly midfield partnership in Kerry's phenomenal run of success.

Lift-off for Jack O'Shea occurred in 1978, with a resounding victory over Dublin in the All-Ireland final. The Kerry machine was fine-tuned to perfection. Jack O'Shea turned in marvellous performances, especially against Roscommon in the semi-final. He and his colleagues ran riot in the final, scoring 5–11 to Dublin's 0–9. Mick O'Dwyer's four-in-a-row team had started with a bang, with the midfield duo of Jack O'Shea and Seán Walsh deserving much of the credit.

'I think Micko realised that we needed a bit of power around the middle of the field and I think we complemented each other,' Jacko recalls of his partnership with Seán Walsh. 'Seánie was a very strong, physical fellow and he wouldn't be renowned for the amount of running he did in matches. Actually, we used to have a slag with Seánie in Kerry that he wouldn't play unless there were 60,000 people watching the match. On the other hand, I would be the mobile midfielder who would do a lot of the running. Funnily enough, he came on at full-forward in the senior team while I played full-forward in the minor team. Yet we both ended up at midfield. We came through the system together as well, which was a great help.

'I think this suited the combination that Dublin had as well at the time. Brian Mullins would be more or less the stationary midfielder who would contest a lot, whereas Bernard Brogan would be the mobile man. That's the way it worked out. I used to be picking up Brogan and Seánie used pick up Brian Mullins most of the time. Seánie was a fantastic fielder, a very strong man, with a very strong upper body, who was able to compete. I'd be looking for the breaks most of the time. We complemented each other in that respect.'

For the four years from 1978 to 1981, Kerry followers made annual pilgrimages to Croke Park for the All-Ireland final. They never came away disappointed. Victory over Dublin in 1978 was followed by a repeat performance in the 1979 decider, when Dublin were defeated by 3–13 to 1–8. The following year, Roscommon were the victims, losing narrowly by 1–9 to 1–6. Nothing, it seemed, could stop this Kerry machine. Croke Park was becoming a second home for the Kerry players and supporters. The stadium's midfield was also becoming a home away from home for O'Shea and Walsh.

'Nothing felt as good as Croke Park when you ran out on to it,' Jacko says. 'There was no pitch in the country that could compare with it. You could feel the difference in your legs. You could feel more of a spring in yourself. This is where I wanted to play. If you can't play in Croke Park, we were told, you can't play anywhere else.

Maybe the pitch wasn't as good as it is today, but the surface was fabulous. It was a dream to run out on to it, just to run out of the tunnel and to hear the crowd. It was enough to raise the hair on the back of your neck.

'A lot of people, including a lot of my team-mates, used to say: "How come you can be so natural and cool?" But I wanted to enjoy those occasions. Even beforehand, I would look into the crowd and if I knew somebody I recognised I would give them a smile or whatever. It was the way I liked to approach it. I wanted to be where I wanted to be and that was out on the field. I wasn't going to let the occasions slip by me. I was out to enjoy them from the word go. And I did enjoy every single one of them.

'I never got complacent. My attitude in football at all times was that I would always meet somebody better than myself. When I did meet them, I accepted it. But I was always determined to go out on the pitch and play with the ability I knew I had, with the amount of strength and stamina that I had. Anybody who wanted to play me would have to play me at my game rather than my playing their game. That was the way I approached things when I got to Croke Park.'

There was something almost pre-ordained about Kerry's four-in-a-row completed in 1981. With the temporary demise of Dublin, the old adversaries were out of the way at least for a while. Offaly made it to the All-Ireland decider, where they were given little chance. The game was tighter than expected. The use of the hand-pass had been curtailed, denying Kerry one of their potent weapons. Pat Spillane was effectively missing, crippled by injury and coming on for only a matter of minutes. However, victory was sealed through a stunning goal scored by no other than Jack O'Shea. It was a long, intricate move, starting in defence and ending in the back of the net. The score was worthy of any of the deadly forwards on the team. Yet typical of that Kerry team, it came from a source that was least expected.

'There was a couple of points in it at the time,' Jacko recalls of that goal. 'The ball went back to our defence, back around the full-back line, and Jimmy Deenihan got the ball. I was outside Jimmy at the time; I was on the 21-yard line under the Cusack Stand. Jimmy moved the ball out to Tim Kennelly, who subsequently, I think, gave it on to Ogie Moran, who gave it on to John Egan. All this time I was making ground up the Cusack Stand side of the pitch and I knew that at some stage this ball was going to come across from the Hogan Stand side.

'At this stage, John Egan was going up the sideline and he kicked it across to Mikey Sheehy, who was 30 yards out from the goal. There was one defender between Mikey and myself. I was coming in from the right-hand side, from the Cusack Stand side. Mikey passed it over his head. Now a lot of people, including Mick O'Dwyer, said I should have given the ball back to Mikey but there was nobody going to take that ball from me. This was my goal. This was going to be my glory. So I just let fly and hit a great shot to the right-hand side of Martin Furlong and hit the roof of the net.

'It was a fantastic move. I think there were seven Kerry players got the ball up to that position before I got the goal. I suppose it's an achievement as well that you've scored in an All-Ireland final. That's the ultimate. But I knew even at 21 yards out from the Kerry goal that if we held possession I could work myself into a position up front to get the ball again. So I travelled that far up the field and I got my just reward at the end.

'It was a great privilege playing at midfield with the players I played with because there was very little selfishness in our team. We worked really hard for one another. The ball was always given to the man in the best position. It didn't matter to us at the end of the day which player was going to put their name up on the scoreboard. It was just that we had to get those scores, we had to use our possession. If we lost possession, we all had to work to win it back. When I went into defence it wasn't because I was told to go into defence. It's just the way you read games. Everybody was given a free licence to play the way they saw it and play the way they wanted to play.

'We hadn't very many tactics in Kerry, like teams might have today. We played the game as we saw it. Wherever we saw space, we hit the ball in. I think it was all down to work ethic from everybody. All of the players on the team and the panel at that time were very versatile and most would have played midfield with their clubs. With Kerry, you played in defence and you played in attack. I think everybody was comfortable playing everywhere else. When we had possession, we all attacked. When we lost possession, we all defended. You could find John Egan back in the half-back line or Paudie Lynch or Jimmy Deenihan up having a shot at goal. Positions meant nothing and I think that was our policy at the end of the day.'

It was John Egan's bad luck to captain Kerry in the 1982 disaster against Offaly, where Kerry lost the chance of a historic five-in-a-row. Ironically, Jack O'Shea narrowly missed out on captaining the team that year. Both he and John Egan played with South Kerry. As county champions, they had the right to nominate the captain. Through a toss of a coin, O'Shea lost out. The following year, O'Shea won the honour of captaining his county only to lose to Cork in the Munster final. The distinction of lifting the Sam Maguire Cup as captain just wasn't to be.

In 1984 Kerry were back with renewed vigour and determination. They cruised through Munster, hammering Tipperary and Cork. They eased past Galway in the championship semi-final, where O'Shea chalked up 0–5. He scored a further point in the All-Ireland final, in a 0–14 to 1–6 victory over Dublin. This was the beginning of Kerry's three-in-a-row won between 1984 and 1986. Almost as important to Kerry, the run of success began in the prestigious centenary year of the GAA. Just as Cork won the 1984 hurling decider, it seemed right that Kerry should take the corresponding football crown.

'Micko was always looking for an excuse every year,' Jacko says. 'From the very beginning Micko was shouting: "This is the centenary year, we have to win the All-Ireland this year." He was always thinking: "What would motivate my men and what would motivate my team?" In '82 it was very hard to be beaten in the five-in-a-row and then the following year we lost against Cork with a minute to go. So the centenary All-Ireland was the motivation in 1984.

'Very early on, I think it was around April in '84, Kerry were down to play two challenge games. One was in Annascaul, where a Kerry team was playing Dublin, and the second game was in County Galway, where Galway were down to play Kerry as well. Kerry had to field two teams on the one day. I won't forget the day because it was the christening of my son in Glenbeigh that morning and I drove to Galway to play the challenge game with the second Kerry team, as we were called.

'The only other established player we had who probably had been playing before that was Jimmy Deenihan. We played Galway with a team of young players who were on the fringe of making it on to the Kerry team. They were the likes of Ger Lynch, Thomas Spillane, John Kennedy and Timmy O'Dowd, and we actually beat Galway that day with our second team. I think the other Kerry team beat Dublin down in Annascaul.

'Shortly after that, there was a trial game probably a few weeks before the Munster final. The A-team that played in Annascaul played the team that played up in Galway in a challenge game. There we unearthed the likes of Thomas Spillane, Timmy O'Dowd, John Kennedy and Ger Lynch. I think this is what the team actually needed at the time because the four-in-a-row team was breaking up a bit and fellows were getting a bit older. We still had the nucleus of a good side and we needed a bit of new blood, and fortunately we picked up those three or four players.

'I think they made a huge difference to us in '84. They all didn't make it on to the team at the beginning, but they were the nucleus we needed in training. Having lost the two years prior to that, they were the inspiration we needed to get us going again. Had we won in '82 and '83, I don't think we might have been there in '84 and '85. I suppose defeat is a bitter lesson at times. It's also a great education. But I think that these new players brought into the panel alongside the established line-up we had, they made us in those three years.'

Jack O'Shea remained with the Kerry senior team long after the glory days ended in 1986. He stayed on for the Cork renaissance towards the end of the 1980s, when Kerry played second fiddle to their age-old rivals. Those were fallow years for a Kerry side that lost to Cork in four Munster finals in a row. Worse was to come in 1992 when they lost to Clare in the Munster final. In a province overwhelmingly dominated by Kerry and to a lesser extent by Cork, the Clare debacle was one loss too many. Following that defeat, Jack O'Shea hung up his Kerry boots.

He did, however, continue to play at club level, first for St Mary's, Cahirciveen, and later for Leixlip in County Kildare. He remained with Leixlip until his retirement in 1997. After a career spanning the latter years of the 1970s and virtually all of the '80s and '90s, Jack departed from the game with seven senior, one minor and three U-21 All-Ireland medals, three National Football Leagues and six All-Star awards. He also was Footballer of the Year in 1980, '81, '84 and '85.

'I look back now and I feel a bit sorry that I made a very harsh decision very quickly after Clare beat us in the Munster final in '92,' Jacko concludes. 'Afterwards, I said maybe I was a bit harsh, maybe I did it too quickly. But, looking back, I don't think I did. At the time it was difficult but now, looking back on it, I've come out of football without any major injuries. I've had a fantastic career, an injury-free career really, which is amazing given the amount of football I played in all corners of the world. I ended up having six or seven more years playing with my club in Leixlip and they were very enjoyable as well. So football has been good to me and I've really enjoyed it.

'I think I was fortunate to be born when I was born. I was fortunate to be brought into the team when I came in at minor level and very fortunate that Mick O'Dwyer and his selectors brought me into the senior set-up. I remember coming on to the scene in '76 and '77 and I was on the fringes of not making it. I think every player goes through that patch. But they stuck with me, they had confidence in me and I ended up making so many friends through football throughout the country. I've enjoyed everywhere I've gone to and played. I would hope that no player holds anything against me. I don't think they could but I hope not. I hope that I left long-lasting memories wherever I played.'

15. COLM O'ROURKE

SPECTATORS AT THE 1988 ALL-IRELAND FINAL MIGHT HAVE WONDERED IF A NEW FORM of warfare had broken out. Fouls, rough play, robust tactics, off-the-ball incidents and a sending-off marred what promised to be an absorbing affair. The original drawn final in September was followed by speculation of reprisals and recriminations. Grim retribution dominated the October replay. For Meath footballers their subsequent narrow victory over Cork resulted in a second All-Ireland in a row. Unfortunately, the price of that victory was a tarnished public perception of the style and tactics of Meath football.

In all four matches with Cork – the 1987 All-Ireland final, the two torrid matches in 1988 and the 1990 All-Ireland decider – one of the game's greatest exponents lined out for Meath. An inspirational player with extraordinarily talent, he became a multiple All-Star and National Football League winner with Meath. He also was voted Footballer of the Year in 1991. The second of his brace of All-Irelands, however, was won in the heat of those 1988 battles with the Munster champions. Along with the rest of the Meath team, he is inextricably linked to his side's battles with Cork fought over a four-year spell at the end of the 1980s and into the 1990s.

'It was a tough affair,' Colm O'Rourke recalls of the 1988 final. 'We had won the league in '88 after a replay against Dublin, which was fairly hot and heavy too. I think the fact that so many of the team were quite old meant that we were hungry for more and more success and we just couldn't afford to wait. By the time we got to the All-Ireland final in September '88 we had been training continually for about two years and I think the edge had gone off the team considerably.

'In the drawn match Cork were much the better team and played with unusual aggression for a Cork team, which sort of took me by surprise. We scrambled a draw, which we didn't deserve on the day's play. The replayed match was played three weeks later. It was well into October when the match was played. Another unusual thing about it was that the weather was still very good.

'We played a bit better but we were much more aggressive physically. I think the root cause of all sorts of problems between Meath and Cork, and probably the perception that the public have of Meath, arose from that match. We steam-rolled our way through the game. We lost Gerry McEntee early on in the match and it was a very physical game. We won by a point, by 0–13 to 0–12, but I suppose it would be true to say that we took no prisoners en route to that title and we didn't win many friends in the media.

'A lot of the Meath players at that time weren't in the business of winning admirers. They went out to win games. Whether they won or lost, they walked away. They didn't try to create any public image for themselves; they didn't try to curry favour with the media. We were painted as the bad boys and we didn't do much to redress that image. Mick Lyons and Liam Harnan weren't the type of players who tried to curry any sort of favour with journalists. There was a lot of the Meath team at that time who were looked on as sort of hard men. We weren't the Muhammad Ali that floated like a butterfly and stung like a bee. We were the black widows, as it were.

'We were fairly ruthless in the way we played. When we set out to play we set out to win. We didn't break the rules but we decided that we'd play to our strengths and our biggest strength at that time was the physical power in the team. In 1987 when we won the All-Ireland we had 13 players who were over six feet tall. They were big, powerful men and they were well able to use their physical advantages. The only problem with Meath being depicted as a very tough team at the time was that it didn't give due credit to the likes of Bernard Flynn, Brian Stafford, Bob O'Malley and Martin O'Connell. They were as good in their positions as any players who ever kicked a football in Croke Park.

'From then on, Meath were treated with a degree of hostility in the press and in the media in general. I think that image of Meath, which was created at that time, has lingered on. I think that the present generation of players are unfairly tarnished because I think the sins of the past shouldn't have been visited on this present group of players. They are much smaller in stature and must rely on their sheer skill and greater athletic power to win games.

'It's funny but life moves on. One of the saddest occasions in Cork was the recent funeral of John Kerins, who was a prince of the game for all those years. No matter what happened in any of those games and no matter who said what, sometimes there were comments made that when you'd look back on them you'd say: "We might have been better off if none of us said anything." There were words exchanged in the heat of battle that sometimes are said and shouldn't be said. But that's the nature of the game.

'Generally, players walk away and there's no hard feelings later. It took something like John Kerins' funeral to bring Cork and Meath players together again. We travelled en masse to show the respect we had for the man. We had a great night along with the Cork team, who I think were very thankful for the fact that we turned out in such force. It was nice to meet them all again because life is too short to harbour any grudges or to carry any gripe against anybody involved in football.

'You must play football in the belief that everybody else is 100 per cent sound. If you have any sort of idea in the back of your head that players have some other agenda apart from just going out and playing in exactly the same way you're going to play, then I think you're better off not playing at all. I have to say I have nothing against anybody I ever played with or against. I think that nobody else has either from that Cork team. It was fairly hot and heavy while it lasted. When you look back on it now maybe it was a bit silly that we should have got so het up over a game of football, but when you had fairly passionate players on both sides you were bound to get that. I think the funeral of John Kerins put all of that to rest and maybe it was about time.'

That day in October 1988 Meath won their fifth senior All-Ireland title and the county's only two-in-a-row. Previous Meath teams had won championship crowns in the 1940s, '50s and '60s, but now Meath joined a select group of counties with back-to-back titles to their credit. As Joe Cassells lifted the Sam Maguire Cup, the Meath players of 1987 and 1988 were elevated to legendary status. Players like Brian Stafford, Liam Hayes, Mick Lyons, David Beggy and

Bernard Flynn became household names. But no star rose faster or no name was more respected than Colm O'Rourke's.

Had things worked out differently Colm O'Rourke might well have ended up playing senior football for County Leitrim and not for County Meath. Although born in County Longford, he grew up in nearby Leitrim close to the Longford border. The O'Rourke family eventually moved to Meath in 1966, by which time three of his brothers had won Leitrim senior championship medals. Within twelve months the young Colm O'Rourke was dressed in Meath colours, cheering his new county to their 1967 All-Ireland success over Cork.

'I remember the game quite clearly,' Colm says. 'It was the first All-Ireland final I was ever at. My brother Pádraig carried me across the turnstile into the old Cusack Stand. That was the time before there were regulations regarding bringing children to matches. I was ten at the time. Seeing Meath win an All-Ireland obviously had an impact but I think an even greater impact was when the cup arrived to my local school in Rathfeigh. Paddy Mulvaney, who was playing right corner-forward at the time on the Meath team, brought the cup to the school and that was certainly a big inspiration. I think at that stage every little boy in that school wanted to play for Meath.

'It was funny that when Meath won the All-Ireland next in 1987 I was the little boy that was playing right corner-forward taking over from Paddy Mulvaney. Strange as it was, there were about four boys in my class and four boys in the class next to me in school and half of those eight played for Meath at some level. So I suppose there was some inspiration came from somewhere along the line.'

Playing for Skryne, Colm O'Rourke soon rose through the ranks and eventually made his début for the club senior side in 1974. In 1975 he began his studies at UCD, where he later experienced Sigerson Cup success. Having played for the county minors, he was promoted to the Meath senior team in 1975, where he arrived just in time for one of the worst slumps in the county's football history. Put quite simply, up to the time of Seán Boylan's arrival in 1982 Meath footballers were awful.

'We went through a valley period in the late '70s and early '80s,' Colm recalls. 'We lost Leinster championship matches to Wexford and Longford which, no disrespect to either county, showed that the level of Meath stock had fallen dramatically. We were in Division 3 South of the league, as it was at the time. We were playing Limerick, Tipperary and Clare and often not even beating them. Things were going badly in Meath.

'As soon as Seán Boylan took over he brought an element of organisation, a great passion to succeed, a hunger and a great camaraderie among the players that had been missing. Things started to improve, but it took us until 1986 to win our first Leinster championship under his reign. For me and for the likes of Joe Cassells, Mick Lyons, Liam Hayes and Gerry McEntee, who'd been playing for almost ten years at that time, that was the real breakthrough in our careers.'

In 1985 and 1986 Meath football stepped up a gear with the discovery of a group of new players that transformed the team. In came names like Brian Stafford, David Beggy, P.J. Gillic, Bernard Flynn, Bob O'Malley, Liam Harnan, Terry Ferguson and Kevin Foley. Combining experienced players with the new arrivals, Seán Boylan's Meath powered their way to Leinster success in 1986.

'That was something that I had always dreamed about as a player,' Colm reflects, 'to wake up on a Monday morning realising that we were after beating Dublin in the Leinster final. I was beginning to wonder at one stage if I would ever play on a Meath team that would beat Dublin. There was a new generation of players that had come in. Most of them had never been beaten by Dublin in a Leinster final so they brought this whole new wave of optimism and enthusiasm and they had no fear of anybody. That created an era of dominance for Meath over Dublin, which lasted for five or six years. It heralded a new era for Meath football and increased the stock of Meath throughout the country.'

In four of the five Leinster finals from 1986 to 1990, Meath became provincial champions by defeating Dublin. Meath made it five titles in six attempts by defeating Laois in the 1991 provincial decider. Not surprisingly their success also spread to the latter stages of the championship. In 1986 they made it to the All-Ireland semi-final, where they lost to Kerry. Then in 1987 they went a step further by beating Cork by 1–14 to 0–11 in the All-Ireland final.

'I can remember that match very well,' Colm says of the 1987 final. 'I can remember nearly everything about the lead-up to the game. Sometimes matches get glossed over and you forget the details, but that was my first All-Ireland and I made a conscious effort to ensure that I remembered everything about it. I remember even the weather in the days coming up to the match. I remember that the Saturday was a very wet, stormy type of day. It rained very heavily and we trained as usual on the Saturday evening and I didn't go out to train. I was feeling a bit off-colour.

'The Sunday turned out to be a beautiful day and a perfect day for football; no wind, a bit of cloud and the ball was dry. I think it was one of the best matches that particular Meath team ever played because we all played well together. Cork started off fairly well and I think they were leading by five points at one stage in the first half. Mick Lyons made a fantastic block-down on Jimmy Kerrigan, who looked to be straight through for a goal. There's no doubt that was one of the major factors that turned that particular game.

'For the next twenty minutes we played some of the best football I was ever involved in with a team. I was lucky enough to get a hand to a ball in the square and it turned in for a goal. Then we had a period of total supremacy in the game. Brian Stafford kicked some wonderful points that day. David Beggy went on one of his trademark weaving runs, sold dummies to everybody, including himself and half the Meath team, and kicked what I think was the greatest point I ever saw in Croke Park. We ended up winning by six points. We played some wonderful football for about twenty minutes. That was the only match between Meath and Cork in that whole time where one side won comfortably.'

In 1988 Meath made it two-in-a-row in the famous ill-tempered clashes with Cork. The team slipped up the following year by losing to Dublin in the Leinster final. Although denied what would have been a famous three-in-a-row, they were far from finished. Meath progressed again in 1990, beating Donegal in the semi-final and once more facing Cork in the Croke Park decider. This time, however, Cork turned the tables on their now long-established rivals, winning by 0–11 to 0–9.

By then, Colm O'Rourke, who was captain in the 1990 final, was established as one of the finest forwards in the game of football. A stylish player, he mesmerised defenders and scored crucial goals and points for his county. In the 1987 final against Cork he scored 1–1.

In the two clashes the following year he scored a total of seven points against the Rebels. His career championship total came to a staggering 16 goals and 105 points.

'I was always playing in the full-forward line,' Colm explains. 'In the beginning of my career I was playing either full-forward or right corner-forward. The quality of Meath forwards in the late '70s and early '80s was not very good so it ended up that I probably scored a lot more at that time than anybody else. I was fairly selfish with the ball anyway so it was probably not unusual.

'When Flynn and Stafford appeared on the scene they were the two greatest scorers that I had ever played with and my scoring rate went down as theirs increased. For the first time I had players with me who were able to score a lot and I often parted with the ball to them because they were more accurate than I was. They also were two-footed players.

'I couldn't understand how any back would allow me to score at all because all I could do was kick with my left foot. It should have been fairly obvious to a back what I was going to do with it every time. Anyway, I used to meet a lot of corner-backs who used to give me the odd point. But I'd say that by the end of my career I was scoring two or three points per game whereas maybe a bit earlier than that I would have been hoping to score a lot more.'

No one will ever forget how the Meath era effectively came to a close in 1991. That year Colm O'Rourke was voted Footballer of the Year. He also shared in Meath's remarkable 340 minutes of football against Dublin in the Leinster championship. That four-game marathon spanned the whole of June and into July, ending on 6 July with a one-point victory for Meath. It was as if Meath's players had given one final collective dying heave before fading off into the sunset.

'I think 1991 was the beginning of the end or even the end maybe,' Colm says. 'If we had been drawn to meet anybody else but Dublin I don't know whether there would have been even a bit of enthusiasm for training. At that stage there were several of the team well into their 30s. The enthusiasm was still there maybe but the bodies were getting weak even if the minds were willing.

'The first game I think Dublin should have won. The second game Dublin should have won. When the thing started to take off it developed great public appeal. But the most enjoyable part of the whole lot was that we didn't have to train much because the games were coming thick and fast and we were able to tick over. Seán Boylan had decided that the best thing to do was very little training and it worked.

'We went off on an infamous weekend to Scotland before the last match. We should probably have lost all the three previous ones but we were still there and we went on a celebration to Scotland the weekend before the last match. The last match was played on a Saturday. We had spent the previous weekend drinking every bar in Scotland dry as part of the celebration for being still there.

'We had great fun. We did a bit of training, of course. We came back and we were lucky to survive the fourth game as well. I think Dublin should have put us away. Keith Barr missed a penalty with about ten minutes to go and we got two goals in the last quarter of the game. We won by a point, with one of the most famous goals I think I'll ever see.

'Kevin Foley never scored, I think, in a championship match before or since. Most people on the Meath team would never have thought he'd ever score in anything in so far as he was a wing-back who was quite happy to stay in that position and never went forward. He ended up on the end of a long passing move which started back at the Canal goal when Martin O'Connell stopped the ball going out wide. It was worked the whole way up and Foley ended up on the end of it.

'He told me afterwards that when he saw the stewards coming out around the field to keep people off the pitch he knew it was time to do something. Every time I see that goal and every time every other Meath person sees that goal, we get a lump in our throat because for me it's the greatest that was ever scored in Croke Park. I think every Dublin man that sees it thinks he's going to cry. If I saw the thing in reverse, having played so well and dominated the game for long stretches and then to be killed off with this sucker-punch, well I think I'd never play football again.'

Colm O'Rourke continued to play football for Meath, eventually retiring in 1995 following his county's defeat by Dublin in the Leinster final. He ended his career with two senior All-Irelands, three National Football Leagues and three All-Star awards. He also managed the Irish side that played International Rules football against Australia at the close of the 1990s. He is best remembered, however, as one of the finest forwards whose love of the game shone through in two decades of championship football.

'Looking back, they were years of fantastic enjoyment,' Colm concludes. 'I think one of the greatest shames of all time is having to grow old because the greatest enjoyment that I ever had in life was playing football. When I was a young fellow I thought I would play forever and now I wish I could because there's nothing beats playing. Everything else and all the things I've done since and all the involvement I have with young teams and coaching, and all the fun and enjoyment I get out of that, totally pale into insignificance compared to being able to play.

'There's no greater satisfaction in life than being able to catch a high ball and turn around and kick it over the bar. Or there's no greater satisfaction than to run out at Croke Park on a big day like a Leinster final when Meath would be playing Dublin or in Navan to play with Skryne in a championship final. Those are the greatest days that you could possibly have. I just wish that some of this cloning could happen where you could extend a player's career and that you could still be playing for Meath when you'd be about 67. It would be just great to be able to do that.'

16. WILLIE JOE PADDEN

THERE IS A BLACK AND WHITE PHOTOGRAPH OF A BLOODSTAINED WILLIE JOE PADDEN
hanging in the hallway of his Castlebar home. It was taken during
the 1989 All-Ireland semi-final against Tyrone. That day, Willie Joe
was forced to the sideline with a dangerous cut to his head. He later
returned to the fray, covered in blood, his head wrapped in a
bandage, his shirt splattered red. It's a legendary photograph in
Mayo, defining the never-say-die commitment of a wonderful player
who gave 14 years to his county yet never tasted All-Ireland
championship success.

That grainy photograph in Willie Joe's hall captures the day when
Mayo qualified for the 1989 All-Ireland final against Cork. Having
beaten Tyrone, the county hoped that a famine stretching back to
1951 might finally end. The ghosts that haunted Mayo teams since
the famous back-to-back All-Irelands of 1950 and 1951 might finally
be banished. Unfortunately, it wasn't to be. Despite an outstanding
display by Willie Joe Padden, Mayo lost to Cork and the career of one
of Gaelic football's greatest fielders ended without an All-Ireland
medal.

'The preparation we put in for '89 was phenomenal,' Willie Joe
says. 'We were prepared first class. We beat Roscommon in the
Connacht final. We played Tyrone in the All-Ireland semi-final and
everybody wrote us off before the game. I got an injury in the game.
I'm not too sure which Tyrone player it was. He was going for a ball
and he hit his knee off my head and I got a few stitches in it. You
don't mind getting a few things like that as long as you win the game.
It was our first experience of getting to a final after all our endeavours
from the previous years. Certainly, from a player's point of view and
from a spectator's point of view, it was a great period because we were

basking in the build-up to the final, especially being in our first All-Ireland final for a long time.

'It was one of the more open All-Ireland finals and it was a very good game of football. Unfortunately, Jimmy Burke, our full-forward, got injured and he had to go off. That really took the wind out of our sails a bit because he was in there as a target-man, and a very good target-man he was. He was very good at winning the ball. We had to kind of re-jig the team. Having said that, we still played very well. We went ahead in the second half. Anthony Finnerty scored a great goal and we were well in the game. But I think somebody got injured and we had to re-jig the team in the last ten minutes. We lost our way because of the changes that had to be made. I couldn't say it was a lack of concentration; it certainly wasn't a lack of fitness because we were as well prepared as Cork. It's just that when we had the initiative we didn't go the extra couple of points up to have the cushion there for the end of the game. Cork rallied and pipped us in the end.

'When you look at it from the perspective of '77 when I started, it was a long time trying to get to an All-Ireland final in '89 and it was very disappointing to lose. It's all right playing in an All-Ireland final but if you don't win no one is going to say who the runners-up were in ten years' time, if they're asked the question. Also very disappointing was the fact that in '89 you were that much older and you were saying: "Am I going to get the chance to stand in Croke Park again and have another go at winning an All-Ireland?" Unfortunately, that didn't happen.'

At the time of the 1989 All-Ireland final, Belmullet's Willie Joe Padden was a seasoned member of the Mayo senior football team. It was 12 years since he had first joined the senior panel, having delivered fine displays as captain of the Mayo minor side that succumbed to Down in the 1977 All-Ireland minor semi-final. Back in the late '70s Willie Joe joined a senior side that was mediocre in the performances it was delivering. The county had fallen a long way from the glory years of the 1950s. Legends like Seán Flanagan, Pádraig Carney and Tom Langan were reminders of great years from the past. The back-to-back All-Ireland titles won in 1950 and 1951 seemed unbelievable when viewed from the perspective of the fallow 1970s.

'I suppose we were lucky in '50 and '51 to win two All-Irelands,' Willie Joe reflects. 'Mayo is a football-crazy county. It was a great era for Mayo football. In fairness to them, the '50 and '51 team were great guys. The effort they put in! To go on and win two back-to-back All-Irelands was a fair achievement. Most of them were from rural parts of the county and it's a big county. How they were able to combine and train I don't know. Certainly, you cannot compare the football of '51 and the football in my time because then you'd rarely see a corner-back coming up the field and scoring a point. Football changed completely, as we all know. But the '51 fellows in their own right made a fabulous contribution to football.

'The players were great. You had Seán Flanagan, you had Tom Langan and you had Pádraig Carney. The one thing they had going for them was that they seemed to be very good leaders. They were very intelligent men. They were able to organise. Seán Flanagan was a great organiser and a very good captain. They seemed to have gelled together and they put in a great effort to do what they did. They are talked about still, whether it is Tom Langan at full-forward or Pádraig Carney at midfield or Seán Flanagan at corner-back. We've had some great corner-backs and some great midfielders and some great forwards since but we just haven't been able to break the mould set by those guys. It was tremendous at the time. They are legends of Mayo football because of what they did for the county. They made a major contribution to Mayo football. It's talked about everywhere you go.'

It was clear in the 1970s that Mayo needed more than a leap of faith to bring back the glory days of the 1950s. The county didn't win one single senior Connacht championship throughout the whole decade. It also goes without saying that Mayo never featured in the final stages of the All-Ireland championship. There were some triumphs at minor and U-21 levels. For example, the U-21s achieved All-Ireland success in 1974 and the minors did likewise in 1971 and 1978. However, the seniors consistently lagged behind their provincial counterparts not to mention counties like Kerry and Dublin that were setting new standards of fitness and performance. It wasn't until the arrival of players like Willie Joe Padden in 1977 that the county began to improve.

'Unfortunately, the '70s were a very lean period for Mayo football,'

Willie Joe agrees. 'We didn't win a Connacht championship in the '70s. But there was a new focus. Kerry and Dublin had set the marker for the previous years. If you were really serious about playing football and if you wanted to be in the All-Ireland series, you went from basically two nights' training a week to four nights' training a week. That's the way it was going, Kerry and Dublin had a marker set. It was just a matter that the training had to be stepped up. We hadn't been doing the training that was required to make a breakthrough at national level. So we went on from there. We got a very good run in the league in '77 and we went on to play Dublin in the league final in '78. It was a very good game. I think it ended up 2–18 to 2–13 and the Dubs won. That was a major step up for Mayo. Mayo hadn't been in a final for a good number of years up to that.'

By the early 1980s the style was back in Mayo football and the county showed signs of reviving its fortunes. From 1981 to 1985 Mayo contested five Connacht finals in a row, winning two. The victory in 1981 carried them through to the lofty heights of an All-Ireland semi-final, where they lost to a magnificent Kerry team that would eventually beat Offaly in the All-Ireland final. Mayo were showing clear signs of a revival, although the loss to Kerry by 2–19 to 1–6 told its own story.

'It was unfortunate in '81,' Willie Joe says. 'We came up against Kerry and they were at their pinnacle. We were probably well in the game at around half-time but in the second half it was no show as far as we were concerned. We got beaten by 16 points in the end. It was disappointing, very disappointing. At the end of the day it might have been a blessing in disguise because it really showed us that we had an awful lot to learn and an awful lot to do to be able to compete with the Kerrys and Dublins of the time.'

Despite their initial hiccups, no one doubted that Mayo were back as a credible football force in the 1980s. They were respected in Connacht and watched with a keen eye by observers from all over the country. The team played football the Mayo way, concentrating on the skills of the game and eschewing robust and aggressive tactics. It was open football, devoid of cynicism and true to the values of honest endeavour. At the core of the team was Willie Joe Padden, battling away at midfield and displaying old-fashioned fielding skills that were fast going out of fashion. A powerhouse in the centre of the park, the only pity was the few chances he had to compete against other great midfielders like Brian Mullins and Jack O'Shea.

'We'd be very open in the football we played and we'd be looking at football as a matter of entertainment as much as winning,' Willie Joe remarks. 'Down through the years we have provided some very good entertainment. Unfortunately, that's no good to you when you want results. But there would be great flair in Mayo football. Maybe you could compare us to the French rugby team to a certain extent. When we play football to our maximum we can be very attractive and play a very good brand of football. There were always some very talented footballers in Mayo, whether it be forwards, corner-backs or half-backs or whatever.

'We always played football with a bit of flair and enjoyment and I think that's portrayed through the club system in the county. Most of the top senior clubs in the county play a good brand of football. It's always encouraged. We're not guys that go out to be negative in the way we play, to be totally concentrating on defending or tackling. We like to show a bit of flair and we have produced good footballers down through the years that had a lot of flair and passion about the game.

'In my era we had some tall men, big guys that we were able to play long balls to. We also had some good fielders like T.J. Kilgallon, Liam McHale and Seán Maher. A few of these fellows were able to catch and win the ball. But the one thing about Mayo football is that we always seem to be able to adapt and play the short game as well. We probably played more of the short game in the 1996 to 1997 era than we played before that. That was because you have to play according to the players that you have on the field on the day. At the time we had a lot of fellows that were very good runners, they were good athletes and were well able to play the short game. But I wouldn't think that we would play any particular brand of football. We were well able to mix it according to what the opposition would require.

'Looking back on it, I modelled my football on Mick O'Connell. He would probably be my idol as regards the style of football he played. He was a tremendous footballer. He oozed with ability and class. Most midfielders would try to model themselves on somebody and that's the person I tried to copy. I would never get to his standard or next or near it, but it was that type of footballer that I would be styling myself on. For a midfielder, I'd be relatively small when you compare me to Brian Mullins, Brian Talty and Dermot Earley and some of the guys that I played against. I'm about 5 ft 11 in. The way I looked at it was that if I couldn't get off the ground there was no point in me being around midfield. I had to rely on the way I could jump off the ground to catch the ball, which thankfully I was well able to do. I just seemed to have a bit of spring in the legs. Maybe I'd have made a good high jumper if I got the right training, I don't know. I could get off the ground. I could jump a few feet off the ground, which was very beneficial to me when you're around the fellows I'm just after describing.

'I could win possession and I was pretty good at it. Looking back on it, you would get a great buzz out of jumping up in the middle of a bunch of players in the middle of the field and catching the ball and coming down. I think it's exciting for the player that's doing it and it's exciting from a spectator's point of view. Unfortunately, that kind of situation is getting less and less because there's more emphasis put on breaking ball. You won't see fellows consistently in the middle of the field dominating and winning clean possession as you would back 10 or 15 years ago. That's the way the game has changed, I suppose. I certainly enjoyed it and I certainly did practise it a lot. It was one of my strong points really. It was probably 80 per cent of the reason why I was picked to play for Mayo.

'It was a privilege at times to go out against Brian Mullins, Jack O'Shea and these fellows because we didn't get out of Connacht that often. When you got out you were looking for the major breakthrough and you were looking at Jack O'Shea and Brian Mullins, Kerry and Dublin. They were in the limelight all the time, so you were looking to be able to pitch yourself against them. You'd be motivating yourself to see how you would compare. It was your chance to get out into the national arena and see how you would perform. I had some good contests with Brian Mullins and Jack O'Shea over a few games where we did meet up. When you got out there you really wanted to say: "Well, am I as good as these guys or am I not?"'

In 1985 Mayo edged tantalisingly closer to a long-overdue All-Ireland final appearance when they drew with Dublin in the championship semi-final. It was a courageous performance by Mayo, who equalised right at the final whistle. Despite leading for a time in the replay, Mayo eventually lost their direction and were defeated by the convincing score of 2–12 to 1–7. That day is recalled for the magnificent fielding of Willie Joe Padden and his battle with Dublin's great midfielder Brian Mullins. The winners met Kerry in the final, where the men from Munster progressed further along the road to a three-in-a-row. For Mayo there were many regrets as the semi-final and perhaps even the final had been there for the taking.

'The one thing that I do remember is that in the drawn game we found it hard in midfield,' Willie Joe remarks. 'We probably broke 50-50 in possession. On the second day we probably had all the possession but we didn't put our chances away and we ended up getting beaten. It was disappointing to have 65 to 70 per cent of the play and still lose the game. I certainly thought it was the best stage of that team. I would certainly have loved to have met Kerry in the All-Ireland final in '85 because I think our team was very good at the time. Certainly, the '84 to '88 period was probably the best period for that team. But we only got to the '85 All-Ireland semi-final and replay.

'We didn't get back to the All-Ireland series until '88 and some of the guys were getting older at that time. In 1986 we played Roscommon in Castlebar in the Connacht semi-final and we had five injuries. We got beaten narrowly and I always maintain to this day that if we had got out in '86 we were well capable of winning the All-Ireland. Kerry contested the All-Ireland that year and were maybe beginning to slow down a bit. I thought it would have been a glorious opportunity but unfortunately we got caught in the province. We got caught by a point by Galway in '87 in Castlebar as well. I wouldn't want to be portraying the hard luck story all the time but we were a bit unlucky that we didn't make the breakthrough.'

Willie Joe Padden and his Mayo team-mates reached the pinnacle of their football careers when they marched out against Cork in the 1989 All-Ireland final. Despite all the near misses of the 1980s, the decade would cruelly come to an end with another courageous defeat. In an enjoyable encounter, Mayo played with their usual football style and panache. They scored a wonderful goal to put them in the lead. Only for the brilliance of Cork goalkeeper, John Kerins, they might have rattled the net on a further occasion. Unfortunately, it wasn't to be and Cork ran out winners by the score of 0–17 to 1–11. Once more, Mayo's dreams were shattered at Croke Park.

The next time Mayo contested an All-Ireland final, Willie Joe Padden was gone from the team. The year was 1996, when Mayo faced Meath in the September showdown in Dublin. There was something familiar in the result of the final, which ended in a draw. What irked Mayo was that the final equalising point for Meath came in the form of a lucky lob that bounced over the bar. The result of the replay was almost predictable. Mayo led at half-time. Meath led at the finish. One again, the championship had delivered a cruel blow to the men from Mayo.

'In the first game we were well ahead in the second half,' Willie Joe says ruefully. 'You have to be subconsciously saying to yourself: "Certainly, this is going to be our year." Then Meath rallied and they ate into our lead. The next thing the ball hops over the bar to level the game. Colm Coyle hit a kick up the field and it hopped over the bar. I haven't seen it happening since. That was disappointing. Having said that, we weren't beaten. But to go back for the replay and to get beaten again by a point, it puts the whole aspect of the ball hopping over the bar into perspective. You would say the chances of that happening in an All-Ireland final are very rare and you would be having a certain amount of doubt as to what you have to do to win the All-Ireland. Wouldn't it have been nice if the ball had hopped for us the right way for all our endeavours down through the years! But that's football, you can't take anything for granted. It's what happens on the day that determines the outcome of the game and it's just that we were unfortunate.'

By the turn of the new millennium, it was just about half a century since Mayo last won an All-Ireland title and there were few indications that victory was imminent. Mayo first won the championship back in 1936. They added two further titles in 1950 and 1951. Back then who would have guessed that a famine would starve the county of further success? Unfortunately for Willie Joe Padden it meant that he seldom displayed his skills at the highest level and, of course, he missed out on winning a coveted All-Ireland medal. With Mayo he won five Connacht senior medals and two All-Star awards. But that was scant reward for a player who, in a career stretching from 1977 right through to retirement in 1992, matched the finest midfield performances ever produced in the game of Gaelic football.

'In 1992 Jack O'Shea had taken over as manager and I suppose his reading of it was that maybe some of the older fellows had enough mileage on the clock,' Willie Joe says regarding his departure from the Mayo senior team. 'He decided to re-jig the whole panel and bring in some new players. My own feeling on it was that I certainly would have contributed for another year or two, maybe as a fringe player or something. But the panel was picked and I wasn't included. It's a shock to the system really when you're involved for so long in Mayo football and the next thing it's not there anymore. You'd be aware every Tuesday or Thursday or Saturday of packing the bags and heading off to training, but that was gone. There comes a time in everyone's career when you have to draw the line and say enough is enough. But you miss it when you put so much into it down through the years. You miss it being away from it. But new managers come in and they pick new panels and you have to move on.

'Looking back on it, if you go through our teams and players we certainly had teams good enough to have won All-Irelands. Whatever it was, we just didn't seem to be able to get the extra little step on the day to give us the edge. It was very frustrating and very disappointing because of the effort that was put in and the amount of talent we had. We were unlucky not to make the breakthrough, but people say that you make your own luck. You can look through 10 or 15 more counties throughout Ireland that didn't make the breakthrough. I'm thinking of Mickey Kearins from Sligo and various other fellows. It would be a nice way to finish off your career. You could always look back and say: "Well, I won the All-Ireland in '89" or "I won it in '85." It would have been the icing on the cake. At the end you'd have something. Unfortunately, it didn't happen.'

17. LARRY TOMPKINS

IT WAS A DAY FOR REVISING THE RECORD BOOKS AT THE 1990 ALL-IRELAND FOOTBALL final. Exactly 100 years before, Cork had won the double by beating Wexford in both hurling and football. In 1900 Tipperary had matched that feat by defeating London in both codes. Now, in 1990, the Rebels defeated Galway in hurling and Meath in football to record the second All-Ireland double in the county's history. That September day the Cork footballers achieved their first-ever back-to-back All-Ireland titles. Cork's Teddy McCarthy became the first man in history to win All-Ireland senior hurling and football medals in the same year. And Larry Tompkins brought a football career that started in County Kildare to culmination when he held the Sam Maguire Cup aloft as captain of his adoptive county of Cork.

'I was lucky to be captain of Cork,' says Larry Tompkins. 'My club, Castlehaven, also had John Cleary and Niall Cahalane but the club made me captain of Cork. It's an outstanding thing to be captain of your county. Not that you have to do anything specifically better or different but it is a great honour and certainly it was a great honour for me to be captain that year.

'We wanted Meath in the All-Ireland like no other team because they had beaten us in a couple of All-Ireland finals. We needed to beat them to really prove ourselves as being a very good side. They came through the other side and we were delighted. We had a lot of motivation going into that game. The hurlers were going great; they had won the All-Ireland final. To go out there on that day and try to pull off something that was going to be historic was something to behold. I'd say the intensity of the last ten minutes of that game for people was just breathtaking.'

Throughout the closing stages of the 1990 All-Ireland final, Larry

Tompkins performed a superhuman feat. In the last quarter of the game he critically damaged the cruciate ligament in one of his knees. Already on painkilling injections for a calf injury, he could barely stand with the excruciating pain. With his medial ligament severed, his leg wobbling and the pain searing through his body, he carried on to the final whistle. That day a battered Larry Tompkins contributed 0–4 of Cork's points in the county's 0–11 to 0–9 victory over Meath.

'There were about 13 or 14 minutes to go,' Larry recalls, 'and I was in a totally accidental challenge with Martin O'Connell underneath the Hogan Stand. I knew I was in fierce trouble and I knew I had done bad damage to my knee. I didn't want to relinquish and I didn't want to come off. I just wanted to make sure that I was on the field to be there to beat Meath. I'd say the momentum of the whole thing just carried me through that day.

'Thank God I survived it and the rest is history. It was a very special day and a very special moment. When you do something like that it sticks in your mind forever more. It was great for the Cork people and it was great for the supporters. People told me afterwards about the intensity of the Cork crowd on Hill 16. I suppose the excitement in the last few minutes, thinking that Cork were going to do the hurling and football in the same year, was something special. There are very few teams from all over the country that can do it and it's a very hard thing to achieve.'

Although from County Kildare, Larry Tompkins grew up sufficiently close to the County Wicklow border that he actually belonged to the parish of Blessington. It wasn't in Wicklow, however, but in Kildare that he made his name as a footballer. From school in Blessington he graduated to club football in Kildare and he was soon on his way through the ranks. A multiple club championship winner with Eadestown, he progressed through the Kildare minors and U-21s and was soon playing for the seniors.

'I started serving my time as a carpenter in Kilcullen,' Larry says. 'From there I used to thumb my way into Naas for training. I was the only one involved on the county team from my club at the time so after training it was a case of thumbing my way back home. I mightn't arrive in until probably half-eleven or twelve o'clock. Sometimes I might have to walk home maybe seven or eight miles. I thought nothing of it because I just wanted to be part of the panel. I didn't see it as hard work. My mum always said to me that I was mad but I just wanted to do my best at the football. I don't think I ever missed a training session and I really enjoyed it.

'I was very happy in Kildare; we had great teams. I played a lot of years with Kildare: three years minor and five years U-21. I enjoyed the football and I enjoyed the lads that I played with. It was great. The support for us was tremendous. At any league game there wouldn't be less than 8,000 people in Newbridge. If you were playing one of the bigger teams you'd be talking about a lot more.'

Unfortunately, what at first was a happy and productive career with Kildare soon turned sour. Having won Leinster U-21 honours and after settling in with the seniors, Larry Tompkins' life took a turn for the worst in 1985. That year was the height of mass unemployment in Ireland. Hordes of young Irish men and women moved to America in search of work. Having recently finished his apprenticeship, Larry's predicament was no different. Out of work for a couple of months, an offer of employment in America was too good to refuse. The offer severed Larry's relationship with the Kildare County Board in a manner that no one could have ever foreseen.

'I finished my apprenticeship in '85 and I was out of work for about 10 or 12 weeks,' Larry explains. 'It was a lean period in Dublin at the time. I was approached by Mick Wright, the Offaly player, and he had contacts in America and asked me was I interested in going there. I was a real home-bird and I didn't want to go but I wasn't working at that time and I said I'd go over and give it a try. So I went over to play with Donegal.

'Kildare asked me back to play in the championship against Meath, in the Leinster semi-final. I had been working nearly seven or eight weeks in America and was employed there and I had to fly over on the Friday and come back on the Monday. I had been out on the All-Star trip so I had the return ticket from that All-Star trip but I needed a return ticket to get back again to the States. They said everything was organised but after the match it didn't seem to be so organised. I was kind of left high and dry and had a lot of difficulty trying to get back to the States because there wasn't anything organised by the Kildare County Board.

'When I went down to the hotel after the match they said that I'd have to pay something like half of the £700-plus for a ticket. At the time any ticket to New York was £400 but seemingly they were late booking it or didn't go about it early enough and this was the only ticket available. Lucky enough, my man in New York, with Donegal, got me on the flight on an Apex ticket for a little over £400 and that was looked after by them.

'It kind of left a sour taste. I had played with Kildare since minor and U-21 and senior, all the way up, and I had been involved with them for eight or nine years at that time. I always gave 110 per cent and never looked for anything. I found it hard to accept at the time and it made me sit up and take notice that they didn't really care. All the players that played with me were very supportive of me and there was a lot of hassle in the hotel towards the County Board.

'I suppose when something like that happens it probably takes a bit out of your heart. However, I've no problem with Kildare. I've got a lot of great mates and friends in Kildare and I just felt sorry at times that I couldn't be there to help them if I was good enough. Every time I see them play and they have success, it brings a tear to my eye. I soldiered a long time with Kildare and that jersey meant an awful lot to me. It's just a pity the way the circumstances went.

'I was over in New York then for a couple of years and I was playing with lads from Castlehaven. There were four lads from Castlehaven with Donegal. I didn't know where Castlehaven was, it could have been in any part of the country but they told me it was in Cork. I got very friendly with them and they always talked about this club. In the spur of the moment it just happened and they asked me would I come back and play with them. I signed a transfer form in January 1987 and I said I'd go back to play with Castlehaven for the summer and see my family, whom I hadn't seen for years.

'At that time there was no mention of playing with Cork or anything like that. It was just a case of going down and playing club football and enjoying a couple of months at home with the family. So that's how it happened. A difficulty then arose with my transfer but it got sorted out and I was transferred to Cork on the day of my birthday, 13 June. The funny thing about it was that I played with Cork before I played with Castlehaven because I was invited up to play a challenge game with Cork against Dublin on that particular day.

'It felt funny that day in Dublin. I remember Frank Murphy coming over to me and welcoming me to Cork. Shay Fahy, who was stationed down in the army in Cork, had transferred to Cork as well and I hadn't seen Shay for years. I had played minor and U-21 with him all the way up with Kildare. It was amazing inside in the dressing-room. Here was Shay putting on a Cork jersey and me putting on a Cork jersey and we were probably two of the most prominent players with Kildare growing up. It was unusual but it was a very proud moment as well.'

Arriving in Cork in 1987 must have been a chastening experience for any ambitious footballer. In the previous 12 years Cork had won just one Munster final and had been beaten by Kerry in each of the remaining 11. If Kerry were the template for success in Munster then Cork footballers were clearly failing the test. By 1987, however, Billy Morgan was building a new Cork team and instilling a new self-belief in the players. The first fruits of Billy's new regime became apparent in 1987, when Cork defeated Kerry in a replayed Munster final.

'Our biggest thing that year was to try and get through against Kerry,' Larry says. 'Kerry had ruled the roost against Cork for a long number of years so I remember that Munster final as a really special day. I had never played in a Munster final before and Páirc Uí Chaoimh that day was chock-a-block and the atmosphere was electric. The lads were telling me that it was their All-Ireland final. Mikey Sheehy getting a goal near the end, when we were two points up, put them a point ahead. Then we got the levelling point, a draw, and the replay was the following Sunday in Killarney.

'The Cork people love going to Killarney and the atmosphere around the streets on Friday and Saturday was just electric. I remember walking down the street the night before the match with a couple of the lads from the Cork team. We went into a pub and the Cork crowd were singing away and I was just like one of them. They were talking about the game tomorrow. I had a great kick out of it for a good half an hour. The whole atmosphere was great and we went out the following day and we won.

'I remember clearly inside the dressing-room afterwards. The bus was outside to bring the team back to the hotel and we were all getting ready. Some minutes later everyone was getting back on the bus and Billy Morgan says: "There's nobody going back on the bus.

You're walking through that town. I walked through that town a long number of years with my head down. I want you to walk through that town today and experience what it's like to win." It was a great feeling and a great moment; there's no doubt about that.

'Then we went on and we were lucky enough to get over Galway in the semi-final after a replay. But in the final, Meath were that little bit more experienced than we were at that stage. They had been there the year before, in '86, and they gave Kerry a great game in the All-Ireland semi-final. There were chances on the day to win it but, having said that, Meath were a good side and they proved themselves afterwards that they were. Losing the All-Ireland wasn't the end of the world. I think Cork's biggest game that year was the Munster final. It was the start of this team and we knew there was better to come.'

Cork's battle with Meath in 1987 set in train an association between the two counties that left its mark on Gaelic football history. In the four years from 1987 to 1990 the teams met in three All-Ireland finals, with Meath winning twice and Cork winning once. In 1987 and 1988 Meath grabbed the headlines with victories over the Rebels, the second after a replay. In 1989 Cork beat Mayo to win the championship crown and the following year took revenge over Meath to make it two-in-a-row. The contests were tough, at times brutal, relations were bitter and no love was lost between the two sets of players.

'It certainly wasn't a love affair anyway,' Larry remarks. 'You start meeting in pressure matches every year. People at the start of the year would be predicting a Cork and Meath confrontation again. I suppose 1988 put the cat among the pigeons, with the rivalry really intense in that game. It was a robust, tough game and Gerry McEntee got sent-off. They beat us with 14 men and the first game was a draw. We had played them a lot of times and it certainly was intense.

'We went on holidays and there was rivalry like in the games. We ended up nearly not talking even though we were staying in the same hotel. We used to be coming down in the elevators together and there would be lads not talking. That was the intensity and that was the rivalry at that time. I suppose with my club Castlehaven we played Skibbereen and there was that same intensity, it's part of the GAA and it's great. But I can honestly say that Meath and Cork guys would say that they were the best years of our lives and we really had the greatest respect for each other.'

Having lost to Meath in the 1987 and 1988 All-Ireland finals, Cork finally cracked the code in 1989, when they beat Kerry in the Munster final and Mayo in the championship decider. That year also, Castlehaven with Larry Tompkins as captain won the county championship. Adding to the pressures in Larry's life was his decision to open a pub in Cork. As it happened, it all came right and 1989 provided some sweet memories for the Cork star.

'Castlehaven were going great in the championship and we advanced to the county final,' Larry recalls. 'Then we beat Kerry in the Munster final and things were really rolling. We played Dublin in the All-Ireland semi-final. We were seven points down and John Cleary got two great penalties and we ended up winning that game and advancing to the All-Ireland against Mayo. Everything was really happening and, as it turned out, we eventually got there.

'It was a difficult year to win an All-Ireland because we had lost you could say the last three, if you include the replay in '88. It doesn't get any easier when you lose a few. There's far greater pressure to deliver then and I felt maybe the team were that little bit nervous. The All-Ireland final was a great spectacle and there weren't many frees in it. There were some great scores and we scored a lot, I think 0–17, but there were tense moments for us as well and we didn't play to our full potential. Thank God, we got through and we got over that iceberg and won that All-Ireland, which we needed to do.

'A few weeks later we won the county championship with Castlehaven for the first time ever. It's a real defining moment because I had come home to play with Castlehaven and to try and win a county championship with them. We have only a tiny population and the people have just one thing and that's football and the football pitch. They love going down there every Sunday to see a match and they longed to see Castlehaven win a county championship. They were close on a few occasions but this was their first time ever to win it. It was a special moment because to be captain of Castlehaven for the first time winning it was really tremendous. That year I opened up a business as well, my bar business, so it was a nice year to be in business with the way things were happening. It went very well.'

Following the 1990 victory over Meath in the All-Ireland final, Larry Tompkins continued to play for the Cork senior football team. By then he had built up a reputation as one of the finest footballers not alone in Cork history but also in the history of the game. In All-Irelands alone his scoring was both deadly and prolific, especially from frees. Not to be outdone, his former Kildare colleague Shay Fahy also contributed to Cork's score-sheets, making the duo the most valuable imports in the Rebel County's long history.

Although a series of injuries eventually helped terminate Larry Tompkins' playing career with Cork, he returned to the side as manager for the 1997 championship. In the following years he transformed the team and eventually led them to successes in Munster while securing a National Football League title in 1999. Also in that year he returned to Croke Park with a Cork team seeking further All-Ireland glory. Having beaten Mayo in the semi-final, who else did Cork face in the final but their old adversaries, Meath. And what else would be at stake other than another potential double following the Cork hurlers' victory over Kilkenny a few weeks before.

'We were really going well that year,' Larry says. 'We had won the National Football League. We had beaten Kerry and a lot of the lads involved in '99 had never beaten Kerry even in minor or U-21. It was a big step to get over Kerry that year. Then we beat Mayo in the semi-final and went on to the All-Ireland final against Meath. I suppose it was unique because the whole thing started to spill over in my head and I felt it was going to be ours again. Unfortunately, it just didn't happen. It would have been tremendous to be involved as a manager with Cork when they would have done the double and to have also done it as a player in 1990. It would have been something special but that's the way it goes, that's sport.'

Throughout his career Larry Tompkins played with Cork in a remarkable four All-Ireland senior football finals in a row. He won two, the second being part of Cork's historic two-in-a-row. As Cork captain, he lifted the Sam Maguire Cup for only the sixth time in the county's history. He also won seven Munster medals to add to his collection and, remarkably for a man from Kildare, he left behind images of a red-blooded, fully committed Rebel playing his heart out for the fans and fellow-players of his adoptive county.

'All my life when I was playing or taking part or getting out there on the field and training, I always wanted to try and do my best and I prepared accordingly,' Larry concludes. 'Some people say I was a fanatic for training but I loved getting out there. To be prepared to do well is very important and getting out there and kicking the balls over the bar or catching or working hard on the field was the enjoyment for me. I wanted to win and I wanted to be the best or I wanted to try and be the best at what I could do. Looking back, the whole thing is about that part of you that needs to win along with the enjoyment of being out there.

'I was lucky in that I came to Cork and got the opportunity to play with a great club, Castlehaven. We had great success. As regards Cork, Billy Morgan was very committed; he gave his whole life to it and still does. He was great and he was probably a bit like myself, being totally addicted to the thing. To be out there playing in major matches and playing in front of big crowds, doing the best you can and really performing and kicking scores, being part of the atmosphere, listening to the *craic* afterwards and talking about players – that's what it's all about.

'The GAA is something special. We can criticise it all we want but both sets of supporters can go to big matches and they can have the *craic* together and they can have the enjoyment. Win, lose or draw, they can go out there and there's not a problem, there's not a hassle and you can look forward to the next day.

'To be a player is the most exciting and the most gripping thing that anybody can be. My family has been very close to me. My mum died recently and it probably took a good chunk out of my heart because she was a great person for the sport. She really was 100 per cent behind me. Every day I went out to play I played for those as well as myself. They were special moments that I'll never forget.'

18. MARTIN O'CONNELL

IT WAS UNDOUBTEDLY THE MOST FAMOUS MARATHON IN THE HISTORY OF GAELIC football. The fixture was a first-round tie in the Leinster championship between Dublin and Meath. It began with a draw on 2 June 1991. The replay on 9 June again ended in a draw. A second replay on 23 June failed to settle the match. In fact, it took until 6 July for the two teams to be separated and even then only a single point decided the contest. In the meantime, some 340 minutes of football had been played. Nine goals and ninety-six points had been scored. A total of almost 250,000 spectators had witnessed the four games. And it all came to a close with Dublin in shock and dismay while Meath quite simply were ecstatic.

'I suppose it was a titanic four games,' Meath's Martin O'Connell, a former Footballer of the Year and a member of the Team of the Millennium, recalls. 'At the start of the campaign no one ever thought we were going to play four games against Dublin. When the draw was made and we were playing Dublin in the first round, everyone was saying it was a Leinster final so early in the year. There was a lot of talk. Everybody was looking forward to it. The players were looking forward to it as well. But it turned out to be four Leinster finals and they were tough battles.

'I remember the end of the first game. I think it was Mick Deegan was coming out solo-running with the ball and David Beggy intercepted it. It hopped in front of P.J. Gillic and P.J. kicked the ball, hoping it would go over the bar. It actually hopped in front of John O'Leary and went over the bar for the equaliser. We were chasing that game from the start. In the second game we were being beaten again and we just battled on and got a draw.

'The only game that we deserved to win was probably the third game. I don't think we deserved to win the last game because Dublin were absolutely cruising. They were winning by five or six points. Then came that famous goal which everybody will always remember, when the ball came from one end of the field right up to the other and it was stuck in the back of the net by Kevin Foley. The ball happened to fall into my hands and we worked it up the field from there. Kevin Foley, above all people, got on the end of it and stuck it into the back of the net to level the match. Then came the David Beggy point and that was it really.

'There were huge celebrations. It was more like a Leinster final. The only thing that was missing that day was that there was no cup. It was every bit as exciting winning that game as it was winning a Leinster final probably because it was Dublin were our opponents. But you'd have to feel sorry for Dublin. Dublin deserved to win three of the games and we deserved to win one of them. I always maintain that they were the better team, but being the better team and being first on the scoreboard are two different things. We were lucky in three games and in the last game we came out with a win. We were just lucky that we were ahead on the scoreboard.'

It wasn't surprising that a player of Martin O'Connell's quality would emerge in Meath during the early 1980s. He was a child in the mid-1960s, when his county exceeded all expectations by producing a rare flourish of football success. Meath powered their way to the 1964 All-Ireland semi-final, where they lost to Galway. That wonderful three-in-a-row Galway team also proved Meath's downfall in the 1966 All-Ireland final. However, the following year Meath defeated Cork to win only their third senior All-Ireland crown. Although not long out of nappies, Martin O'Connell was unlikely to have escaped his family's euphoria at this extraordinary triumph. It was, after all, a football-mad family and, right from the start, his parents immersed him in the culture of Gaelic football.

'From the beginning, when I started playing first at U-8 level my father brought me everywhere,' Martin says. 'My father and my mother were into football. Wherever football was I was at it. We were kind of a footballing family really. I remember playing U-12 and I was only eight at the time and I had no football boots of my own. I had to get a brother's boots. I think they were size six or seven. I think I had to put four or five pairs of socks on my feet to fit the boots. That's back a long time ago.

'Eventually, I got on the Meath minor team and I was lucky enough to get on that. I went from that to the U-21s and then on to the senior side. But the club had a big role to play, it helped me out an awful lot as well, with different fellows bringing me to challenge matches and bringing me to trials and all that type of stuff. The club did a lot for me that way. But at that time there was really nothing, only football. It was football no matter where you went. Nowadays, there's a lot of other activities and other sports, but at that time it was football seven days a week.'

Like so many talented footballers, Martin O'Connell could perform in a variety of positions. In that sense alone, he was a dream come true for Seán Boylan, who took over as Meath manager in 1982. Martin had already played with the Meath minor team and clearly showed promise. Boylan brought him straight into the senior squad, where he was tried at corner-forward. In time, Martin was moved to his favourite wing half-back position, although annoyance at being shifted elsewhere in the team led to his brief resignation from the panel. Those hiccups in the relationship between player and manager were temporary, however, and it was as an attacking wing-back that Martin O'Connell forged his illustrious career, culminating in his selection on the Team of the Millennium.

'I think every new fellow that comes in starts off as a corner-forward and he's taken off this game and tried the next game,' Martin says. 'Eventually, I got settled in as a wing half-back. I preferred to play there and it went from there. I think it's maybe an easier position to play in because you're facing the ball. I also had a lot of good men around me, which made my job fairly easy. I had a little bit of a mishap in '87 when I left the panel because I wasn't getting a place as a wing-back. I was played up front. It was probably the sorriest thing I ever did, but I was glad that Seán rang me and we made up and I got back in the squad.

'When you are playing up front, you kind of have to be a natural forward. When you go back to all the great teams that Dublin, Kerry or Meath had, I don't think you could see Colm O'Rourke or Bernard Flynn or Mikey Sheehy playing as a back. They are only three examples. I think you have to be a natural to play as a forward and I don't think I was a natural forward. I preferred to play in the backs and I preferred meeting the ball with good backs around me.

'I just loved the position. If you didn't like your position you'd probably be worried about what was going to happen. But as a left half-back I was fairly comfortable and I liked the position. It made it that bit easier so I didn't fear anybody. I was very serious about training and about playing. If we had a challenge match, I would treat it as a Leinster final or as an All-Ireland final. It's just the way I was. It didn't bother me who I had to mark. He was just another man. He had two arms, he had two legs and that was it. Names or anything like that didn't really put me off from marking anybody.'

Nowhere was the quality of Martin O'Connell's football prowess more evident than in the 1987 and 1988 All-Ireland campaigns. In both years' finals, Meath faced opposition from Cork. It was a strange set of opponents, with Cork replacing Kerry as representatives from Munster and Meath taking the place of Dublin as Leinster kingpins. In particular, the 1988 final and replay are recalled as bitter, controversial, rugged affairs, with Meath's Gerry McEntee being sent off in the latter game. In all three final matches Martin O'Connell laid claim to being one of the finest half-backs in the contemporary game. In particular, he delivered an exemplary and passionate performance in the 1988 replay. In those two years he also won his first two senior All-Ireland medals.

'There was a lot expected of the Meath team,' Martin says of the build-up to the 1987 All-Ireland final. 'In '86 we were kind of happy enough with winning a Leinster. Then we were lucky enough to get back and win a Leinster again in '87. But we wanted to go on that step further and win an All-Ireland semi-final and win the All-Ireland, and that's what we did. We didn't fear anybody. We didn't really know much about Cork because it was always Kerry that was coming up from Munster at that time. Now Cork were after beating Kerry and we respected them and we knew it was going to be tough.

'Regarding the game itself, we didn't start off that well. I think we were five or six points down. I remember Jimmy Kerrigan coming up the field and Mick Lyons from point-blank range blocked the ball and that gave us a bit of a lift. From there on, we never looked back. We tagged on a few points. We got a goal from Colm O'Rourke and at the start of the second half we banged over three or four points. We won that game comfortably in the end.

'In '88 we were hungry enough to try and win back-to-back All-

Irelands. Again it was Cork, who had made a few changes on the All-Ireland team. We wanted to win two in a row and we were lucky. It went to a replay. We were lucky the first day and the second day we lost a man early on in the game. We just pulled out all the stops and we got there in the end. We knew that it was going to be difficult because a team that was after losing an All-Ireland the previous year to the same opposition was always going to be tough. And it was tough.

'I think the bitterness was blown out of all proportion. I suppose the media didn't help and maybe the players on both sides were a bit stupid and foolish with their carry-on. We went abroad on holidays and some of us were staying in the same apartments as the Cork boys. They were at one side of the pool and we were at the other side of the pool and nobody wanted to move. One team was thick and the other was twice as thick. We should have met and said: "Lads, let's forget about this and enjoy our few drinks and have a bit of *craic*." But that didn't happen, and it went on for a long time.

'Papers were writing about this, that and the other. Gerry McEntee being sent off was another issue; you'd think he was after killing somebody in the All-Ireland that year. He wasn't the only man to be sent off in an All-Ireland final and he wasn't going to be the last. I suppose it was all a bit stupid but, having said that, it passed. We hadn't seen each other for years and years until the sudden death of John Kerins. A lot of us went down both to the removal that night and to the actual funeral on the day. We had a few drinks and we talked and we chatted and everything was back to where it should be. Unfortunately, it took a death like that to make it normal again. That type of stuff shouldn't have happened. Thankfully, it's gone now.'

The success of Meath continued in the following years, when they won two further Leinster titles, reached another two All-Ireland finals and won the National Football League. In 1989 Dublin blocked their path to the final stages of the championship by defeating them in the Leinster final. The following year Meath won the Leinster title and reached the All-Ireland final but lost to Cork. They also won the National Football League in 1990. In 1991 they added another Leinster title to their collection and reached the All-Ireland final but lost to Down. It was a truly remarkable era for what was undoubtedly the finest collection of players ever to turn out in the green and gold of Meath.

'I think there was a bit of everything in that team,' Martin remarks. 'There were a lot of good footballers and there was a good mix. We had three backs that were able to play the ball and I was one of those. Then you had three men, Mick Lyons, Liam Harnan and Kevin Foley, who could play ball and do a little bit of the rough stuff, if you like to call it that, and they helped us in the backs. Then you had the two boys at midfield, Gerry McEntee and Liam Hayes, who I thought were outstanding for Meath. They were probably the two best midfielders in the country for those four or five years. Then up front you had Colm O'Rourke and Bernard Flynn and P.J. Gillic, who did an awful lot of work that you wouldn't really see him doing. He did a lot of hitting and could play the ball as well. You had Brian Stafford taking frees. David Beggy was liable to do anything; we didn't know what he was going to do and the opposition didn't know what he was going to do. It was kind of a blend and a mix and it worked well.'

Although Meath added a further National Football League to their collection in 1994, their performances in the championship were hardly inspiring. In fact, it wasn't until 1996 that Meath would rise again. By then, the vast bulk of the late 1980s side was gone. Colm O'Rourke, P.J. Gillic and Brian Stafford were out following a massive defeat by Dublin in the 1995 Leinster final. There were two exceptions, however, as Colm Coyle and Martin O'Connell remained in the team. With new players like Trevor Giles and Graham Geraghty, and with Martin O'Connell a rock at the back, Meath went on to beat Mayo in the All-Ireland final replay. It was Martin O'Connell's third All-Ireland medal. He won his fourth All-Star that year. He also was selected as Footballer of the Year for 1996.

'I suppose '96 was a whole new team,' Martin says. 'Colm Coyle and myself were lucky enough to stay on for that year and it turned out to be a great year. It was a totally new set-up. You had new players apart from maybe two or three on the team and three or four maybe in the subs. I always knew that Meath would come back at some stage to win an All-Ireland. I just didn't think it would be so soon, especially after being beaten by ten points by Dublin in '95 in the Leinster final. That was a real kick in the teeth and a lot of lads left after that. We came back with a new team and to win an All-Ireland was unbelievable.

'I remember going up to play Carlow in the first round that year and everybody in the county gave us no chance. A lot of players felt a lot of pressure going up to play Carlow because I think Éire Óg were in the All-Ireland club final. I think there were nine or ten of that team on the Carlow team and we were worried going up. It turned out that we beat them easily and then we started to think that this team could go places. We played Laois in the following game and we won again. There was a bit of fight coming into the team. We went from strength to strength. We played Dublin, who were All-Ireland champions, in the Leinster final and we beat them by two points. Everything was knitting nicely. We played Tyrone in the All-Ireland semi-final and beat them easily and it took us two games to beat Mayo. Overall, it was a fantastic year.

'Things had changed. The whole game had changed; the quick frees, the line-balls out of the hand, it was all speed. In '87 and '88 everything was put on the ground. Free kicks were on the ground and maybe it was slower. So it is very hard to compare the '87 and '88 team to the '96 team. But '96 turned out to be a fantastic year. Going back again to '95, after being beaten by Dublin by ten points to come back and to achieve what we achieved in '96 was fantastic. There was an All-Star and Footballer of the Year and overall it was fantastic, especially when early on in the year nobody gave us a chance. I'd even say some of the players didn't think we'd do it again.'

It took until 1999 for Meath to win another All-Ireland final and by then almost one-half of the victorious 1996 team had disappeared. Seán Boylan was still in control of team affairs and still demonstrating his ability to mould and transform Meath footballers into All-Ireland winning sides. The four All-Irelands won since Boylan took over in 1982 were nothing short of remarkable. Unfortunately, players had to come and go to fuel this level of success. In 1998 it was Martin O'Connell's turn to depart. Now crippled with back problems, his time in a Meath senior shirt had come to a close.

'I had an injury to my back, that was the start of it,' Martin says regarding the end of his career. 'I had a disc removed in '97. We

trained the Tuesday and Thursday nights before the Leinster final in
'97 and there wasn't a bother on me at all. I got up on the Friday
morning and I barely could get out of bed. I was in so much pain in
my back and down my leg. I went to Seán Boylan and Seán told me
to go to the team doctor and we would see how I was in the morning.
On Saturday morning I couldn't move. It was unbelievable pain. I
didn't know what it was. I got pain killing injections and thought
they'd work but they didn't work.

'It was only about three or four days after, when I was brought
into the hospital, that I realised what it was. It was a disc lying on a
nerve and I had to have an operation about a month later. That really
was the end of it. I tried to get back in '98, played a few challenge
matches and trained with the county right through the league. But I
just never really got back on the team in '98. So I finished up. I was
on the panel in '98 but never really made the team. That was it,
really.'

When the Football Team of the Millennium was announced, the
only player from modern times to be named was Martin O'Connell.
To be listed alongside great names like Mick O'Connell, Seán Purcell
and Seán O'Neill was a rare honour indeed. It was probably the
ultimate tribute that could be paid to this extraordinary attacking
wing-back, who had played such an influential role in three of his
county's All-Ireland successes. He was, as the Team of the
Millennium administrators pointed out, unique in Meath as the only
player to hold three All-Ireland medals and six Leinster
championships. Added to his three National Football League medals,
his four All-Star awards and his Footballer of the Year trophy from
1996, it was an appropriate haul of silverware for one of the finest
half-backs in the history of Gaelic football.

'That was a surprise, to get on the Team of the Millennium,'
Martin concludes. 'I suppose you have controversy no matter what
team you play or pick. If it's only a club team or a county team you
pick, there's going to be controversy over it. For me to be on the
Team of the Millennium was fantastic. It didn't really sink in maybe
for a week or two after. There were so many great players and to be
named as one of them was nice, I suppose. But you could pick ten
different teams and still have controversy.

'I'd do it all again. I have no regrets at all. It was fantastic. There were great times. I met great people and I travelled a good bit of the world. I just had one bad injury in my back and really that was all. I broke my hands as well and a few ribs but that was it really. I started my own business as well, probably because of the football. I probably wouldn't have started it up if I hadn't been playing football. So it was good, football was good to me and I hope I was good to football. Maybe I was, maybe I wasn't, but I enjoyed every minute of it.'

19. MARTIN McHUGH

LITTLE DID THE GREAT SAM MAGUIRE REALISE THAT ONE DAY HE'D FLY BY
transatlantic jet all the way to Chicago. Having died in 1927, this
former player and administrator could never have foreseen how it
might happen. After all, he had barely witnessed the first attempts at
transatlantic aviation. Flying by jet-propelled engines at an altitude
of between 35,000 and 40,000 feet was, understandably, an
unimaginable dream. But that's precisely what happened. Not long
before Christmas 1992, there sat Sam, occupying his own seat,
perched between Donegal's Martin McHugh and Anthony Molloy,
flying all the way to Chicago.

It was of course 'Sam' as in Sam Maguire Cup that sat propped in
its own seat on that trip to the United States of America. Sam also
went on to New York, Boston and Philadelphia. The trophy had
travelled before, but this time the occasion was to celebrate Donegal's
first-ever senior All-Ireland triumph. The purpose of the trip was to
share with emigrants from the hills, valleys, towns and fishing
villages of Donegal a success they had patiently awaited for over a
century. Some might remember Ulster finals from the '60s, '70s and
'80s. Others might recollect earlier disappointments and failures.
None could recall anything to match that sweet September day in
1992 when Donegal beat Dublin to win the county's first All-Ireland
senior championship title.

'Anthony Molloy and myself went out to the States with Sam,'
Martin McHugh recalls. 'It was great. First of all, Sam got a special
seat on the plane. Also, way back when you were younger you
sometimes had problems going through emigration but when we
landed in America they pushed us through with Sam and they
wanted photographs with Sam. It just showed what Sam meant to

everybody. It was great for the Donegal people in the States. You'd walk in and you could see them coming up beside you and straightening up their shoulders. They were so proud that Donegal were taking out Sam and they probably never thought they'd see it.

'We did Chicago, Boston, Philadelphia and New York and it was great just to see it. I think it meant more to those people. They were there when Kerry took out Sam and they were there when Dublin took out Sam and when Offaly took out Sam and Down and other different counties. It was great for them; they were so proud. It was great for people that were away, what it meant to them, and we were hearing the stories about "how much money we won on you" and all that. It was the exact same thing when I went over to England. It was very proud for us and the memories will stick.'

Sometimes a sporting victory means more than the winning of a trophy or the securing of a national title. Donegal's first-ever All-Ireland victory in 1992 belongs to that category. Although the county always prided itself on its Gaelic football traditions, decade after decade its footballers returned disappointed from championship campaigns. Isolated in the rocky north-west corner of Ireland and facing into the fierce Atlantic, Donegal was as geographically remote from the rest of the country as its footballers were from their counterparts in Kerry and Dublin. To put it bluntly, Donegal was seen as something of a Gaelic football backwater.

In the 1980s Donegal's image started to change. In 1983 they won the Ulster championship, beating Cavan. In 1989 they lost the Ulster final to Tyrone after a replay. The following year they beat Armagh, securing another coveted Ulster crown. In 1991 they again reached the Ulster final, losing to Down. Throughout all that time, Donegal became real contenders. Their team contained many talented players, none more wise and astute than their U-21 All-Ireland winner in 1982, Martin McHugh. A soon-to-be Footballer of the Year, back in 1991 and early 1992 he and his team-mates had yet to truly emerge from the sporting shadows.

'We were hammered by Down in '91 in the Ulster final,' Martin recollects. 'We came back in '92 and we played Fermanagh in the Ulster semi-final and we played poorly. We were meeting either Down or Derry in the Ulster final. They were playing the following Sunday in the other semi-final. We felt that how things were going in the county with training and with everything else, it wasn't going to be good enough. We had a meeting after that match and I think that's the day we made the decision in the dressing-room that we were going to give this a go. We, the players, kind of had a meeting ourselves. We asked for the training to be upped and we asked every player to give a total commitment.

'We had beaten Cavan after a replay in the first round and then we played Fermanagh, so we hadn't really to peak until the Ulster final. I think definitely that day was the day we made the decision. Players pushed each other on after that. There was a different attitude at training and a different attitude everywhere. I felt that gelled the whole thing together and probably won the All-Ireland.'

Following victory over Derry in the Ulster final, Donegal faced Mayo in the 1992 All-Ireland semi-final. Donegal won that day, beating Mayo by 0–13 to 0–9. In the other semi-final Dublin beat Clare by 3–14 to 2–12. As the final approached all bets were on Dublin, who, it appears, were bubbling with self-assurance and were confident of success over their less salubrious rivals. The facts were simple: Dublin were going for their twenty-second championship title while Donegal were going for their first. It seemed stupid to bet on the outcome.

That September day in 1992, fans from the north-west brought with them all the excitement and enthusiasm inevitably linked to a county's first All-Ireland appearance. Dublin was awash with the colours of Donegal. In contrast, Hill 16 was a sea of blue. Dublin's optimism and Donegal's apprehension seemed justified when news filtered through that Donegal player Martin Shovlin was out through injury. Injured or not, the game would go on. Led by captain Anthony Molloy, two Donegal brothers ran out on to Croke Park that day. They were James and Martin McHugh. It was the beginning of an extraordinary odyssey that would win All-Ireland medals and All-Star awards for both brothers while older brother Martin would also become Footballer of the Year.

'The hype in the county was unreal,' Martin recalls of the build-up to the final. 'I think the thing that saved the players from a lot of it was the tickets. Most people's biggest problem was tickets. Instead of worrying about whether the team was going to win in Croke Park or anything else, all people were asking for was tickets. That was really something we didn't expect but it happened. It was put in the local papers and in the local media to leave the players alone, not for anybody to ask them for tickets or anything else. It took the pressure off and I think that definitely helped.

'The other thing is that two weeks before the All-Ireland final we went together to Letterkenny and we stayed overnight in Letterkenny as a team and then we played a match down in Milford. That day we also watched the All-Ireland hurling final on television. We didn't really watch the match but we watched the build-up because it's completely different where the teams come out early and everything else. Things like that were very well worked out.

'Also, we were underdogs going into the match and there was no pressure on us. Everybody in the country, bar Donegal people, said we were going to be beaten. A lot of people in the county were just happy that the team was in an All-Ireland final and they were going to enjoy the occasion. Looking back on it now, the pressure was completely off us, which was good from the team's point of view. We were in the All-Ireland and people didn't realise that we were a very experienced team because we had been around a long time.

'I think the important thing is your own mental preparation. I knew what I was going to do. I was going to get out there on the field, soak up the atmosphere and take it in. We had plenty of time. In an All-Ireland semi-final you're only out on the field and you're nearly ready to play whereas in an All-Ireland final there's no point psyching yourself up because you've got to relax, you've got to meet the President and other different things. It takes a good while to do it. I had gone up to the Clare–Dublin semi-final in Croke Park, and the only thing I watched during that match was Keith Barr. At the start, Francis McInerney offered him his hand and Keith didn't take it. He had won the first battle. I wasn't going to offer Keith my hand, just to make sure. They are simple enough things but I think they're very important. I got myself mentally right that way and that's why I felt strong.

'We had our homework so well covered that we actually knew what side of the field John O'Leary's kick-outs went. We knew where they were going to go, so everything was covered. There's a lot of that in Gaelic football now but at that time there mightn't have been as much of it. We also kept saying that we wanted to crown Anthony

Molloy as "King of Donegal". That was the motivation we used; that we wanted to see him going up the steps. And we thought about what it would be like sitting down on the field watching the Dublin captain going to collect the cup. It all worked for us.

'The night before, in the hotel, we knew that Martin Shovlin was struggling and he did everything in his power to make it. I wouldn't like to say how many injections he got. It was a blow, but the one thing about it was that the squad was strong. It was very hard on Martin to make the decision but, in fairness to him, he made the decision that was right for the team. At that time you were only allowed three subs, so if you had to go off after five minutes you were a sub down. John Joe Doherty came in and played very well, which was a plus. But when we look at that team we always say that Martin Shovlin was on it.

'People say that if ten of the players play well you'll win a match, but we look back at that All-Ireland final and I'd say that the sixteen players that played all played well. That's what it takes to win an All-Ireland. It just went right for us and clicked for us on the day. People won their own corner and I think it's important in Gaelic football that people win their own corner. That day we also had leaders on the pitch. We had people taking on responsibility, which is very important. But if we look back on it now, the fact that Manus Boyle was kicking every free over the bar was vital. When we look at rugby nowadays, or any sport, it's important you score your frees and Manus was kicking every free we got that day.

'We had a spell when everything went right for us. We won the game during that spell about ten minutes before half-time. We started running at Dublin and we kicked a lot of very good scores. The other decision we made was that if Anthony Molloy won the toss we were going to play in to the Hill, we were going to give Dublin no advantage. Maybe if Dublin's Charlie Redmond had got his penalty in to the Hill it would have been different. As it happened, his penalty miss had a big bearing on it. We had to test them every way, especially us being the country team, and we felt that one way was to test their supporters early on by playing in to the Hill.

'I was so confident beforehand that we were going to win the All-Ireland that I said the one thing I was going to do when the final whistle went was to get the ball. I wanted the All-Ireland ball. I think

Tommy Sugrue, the referee, wanted the ball as well. Just at the end he blew the whistle and he caught the ball off Declan Bonner, who had gone down the ground. I grabbed the ball off him and he wouldn't let it go and I wouldn't let it go. The next thing the crowd started coming on the field and I kept holding on to it and he kept holding on to it. I got it in the end and held on to it.

'The next person out to me on the field was my own wife, Patrice, which was great. After that, I don't remember a lot. The next part I remember is going into the dressing-room afterwards and sitting down and thinking about what I achieved. The word came through that Joyce McMullan's brother, who was sick, had died. It was a rumour and that put a big damper on the whole thing. From winning the All-Ireland, everything went dead in the dressing-room. But his sister came in later and said it wasn't true. After that, everything else was just hype and more hype.

'That night we were out in the Grand Hotel in Malahide and the celebrations were great. Daniel O'Donnell was out singing and the whole of Donegal was there. It was great out there. Then we came back by train to Sligo and I think there were 10,000 to 15,000 people in Sligo alone to meet us. That's when it starts to sink in what you've achieved. We went to Bundoran and then Ballyshannon and then into Donegal town. And the crowds! I never witnessed anything like what was in Donegal town that night.

'The one thing I remember was when we were up on the stage and they started singing "Simply the Best". The hair stood up on the back of my head. When you looked down you saw people crying, and even talking to people that night everybody was so happy. Older people were saying they could die happy now. What I said that night was that I was going to enjoy the week and I went to every club with Sam. I went everywhere and it really was something to see the different people. It put a great smile on people's faces. Football can do that, and it's great.

'The most important thing at that stage from my point of view was winning an All-Ireland medal. I was 31 that year and it was a great year for Kilcar club and a great year for the McHugh family. It was great to have the two of us playing on the half-forward line and the two of us winning All-Stars as well as getting the All-Ireland medals. We were attending functions everywhere. For the two of us, the proudest moment we had was when Sam stopped outside our own house and all the people of the Bavin town-land were all there greeting Sam. Then we took it down to Kilcar. When we went down, the Kilcar pipe band was out to lead James and myself with Sam down the town, and that was great. That's something we will never forget.'

For the record, Donegal beat Dublin by 0–18 to 0–14 to win the 1992 All-Ireland final. It was a day when Martin McHugh produced one of his many fine performances in a Donegal shirt. It also was a day when many players from Donegal's victorious U-21 All-Ireland winning teams of 1982 and 1987 achieved the pinnacle of success with the county's senior side. Significantly, it was the second All-Ireland title in a row for a side from Ulster, with Donegal replacing Down as worthy champions.

Ironically, it was another Ulster team that would displace Donegal as All-Ireland champions in 1993. A tired Donegal side dragged its way through the National Football League, which began shortly after the championship had concluded. Donegal lost in the final to Dublin, in a replay. An Ulster championship semi-final victory over Armagh set up a provincial decider against Derry. But that day, stuck in the muck in Clones, Donegal relinquished their Ulster crown and opened the door for Derry's subsequent first All-Ireland success the following September.

'We had to come back playing football in October whereas now they've got the break until February. That makes a big difference,' Martin reflects. 'We were celebrating, partying and playing and we were able to do it because it was happening on confidence. I remember the team going down to play Carlow one night in a match. The team went down and I didn't go down until the following day. They were up at a disco and they were partying and we went out and we beat Carlow by maybe 15 points the following day. But the problem was that we picked up a lot of injuries and that was a worry.

'It was a very wet day the day we played Derry, although I think that Derry were knocking on the door anyway. The year before, they were favourites to beat us in the Ulster final, so we look on it that they deserved their All-Ireland. It was great and we had great battles with Derry at that time. There was great rivalry between us, no love lost on the field but great respect and that's what it's all about. But it was disappointing when you look back on it. When we look at it now, I think we won the first All-Ireland too late. The team got close enough to breaking up after that.'

Throughout his career, Martin McHugh was always referred to either as 'The Wee Man from Kilcar' or 'The Wee Man from Donegal'. His stature, however, had little bearing on his powerful and blistering contributions to his county's successes. Having arrived on the senior side in 1980, he was part of the county's All-Ireland triumphs at U-21 level in 1982 and at senior level exactly ten years later. An All-Star in 1983 and 1992, he later coached the Cavan senior football team. He also won the treasured title of Footballer of the Year in 1992. But it's for his role in Donegal's historic All-Ireland success that Martin McHugh will always be remembered. No other player could better his contribution to Brian McEniff's wonderful team. Nor could any player lay claim to a more influential role in banishing forever the ghosts of failure from Donegal football.

'Everywhere we go, people talk about '92,' Martin concludes. 'I know if you're involved in the county team at the minute, you'd like to say: "Forget '92, let's move on." But I think it's great and it's great to meet the lads and look back on it. At times, my own wee fellows would put on the video in the house and you'll watch it and you'll see something you didn't see the last time you watched it. I get people ringing my house looking for the video of that match because they want to show it to youngsters to point out that this is what can be done, especially by a team going in as underdogs. Maybe people will say it very seldom happens in Gaelic football. It can happen in soccer because you can get a goal and hold out. Definitely it was very important from that point of view and I think the belief that you can do something is very important. We proved that we could do it as underdogs.

'Looking back on it, from a personal point of view what was important was the enjoyment and the satisfaction it gave, the enjoyment that it gave to my family and the enjoyment it gave to my club. From a Donegal point of view what mattered was what it meant to the people of the county. I think somebody said that there was no cow milked in Donegal for so long afterwards. The enjoyment was all over the county; it was everywhere you went. I don't think I'll ever forget people saying they'll die happy after a football match. That was what it meant, especially to older people.

'But the one thing that I'd like to always remember is the amount of people that played for Donegal and that never won an All-Ireland. I was one of the lucky ones to be on that team and to win one. I think it's important that we remember the amount of people, better footballers than ever were on that team, who didn't win an All-Ireland. It's important we remember them because they have done as much. It's just that we were lucky enough to make the breakthrough.'

20. ANTHONY TOHILL

ON MONDAY 20 SEPTEMBER 1993 A MASS OF PLAYERS AND SUPPORTERS CLAD IN RED and white left Dublin for their victory march to Derry. They were like a triumphant army returning with the spoils of war. They edged north through Drogheda and Dundalk, crossed the border near Newry and then headed for Armagh. Veering north-west to Dungannon, they made for Cookstown and finally arrived in Maghera. It was, in truth, an unexplored route. For the first time ever the greatest prize of all, the Sam Maguire Cup, was being brought home to Derry.

A Derry team came close before, losing in 1958 to Dublin. Other Derry sides won Ulster titles in the 1970s and '80s yet failed to wrest the ultimate prize. But now this army of Derry players and supporters returned from the scene of battle as champions for 1993. There were many new legends created during Derry's march to All-Ireland success. Names like Joe Brolly, Enda Gormley, Henry Downey, Kieran McKeever and Tony Scullion, amongst many others, had made their mark. But none outshone the towering midfielder who inspired Derry's greatest-ever year: a player by the name of Anthony Tohill.

'I remember it being a very long day,' Anthony Tohill recalls of that famous homecoming in September 1993. 'Every town we went through we were stopping, such was the warmth and hospitality of the people that we met. We finally came into Maghera at about three o'clock in the morning to be confronted by about 30,000 people. It was amazing and it was a marvellous occasion. You could never have expected that it would have created so much buzz and that there would be so much warmth and so many congratulations from counties we maybe would have looked upon as being our rivals in sport. The people of Tyrone, Down and Armagh gave us a great reception. It was a marvellous occasion and something that the people on the bus that day will never forget.

'I recall one particular incident when we were going through Cookstown. The place was lined with people. I can specifically remember one older man, he must have been maybe 80 years of age and dressed in a wee cap. He carried a little red and white flag and he was waving this flag and the sheer delight that was in that man's face as he walked! He must have walked nearly the entire length of Cookstown's main street, which is one of the longest main streets in Ireland. What it must have meant to that guy I can only imagine. I'm sure that it meant so much more to him than it did to a lot of the people sitting in the bus. This guy had probably lived his whole life associated with football and GAA in Derry and probably never thought that he'd see in his lifetime Derry winning an All-Ireland. It was very nice to know that along with winning the actual trophy we also brought so much joy to that person. Seeing him and his reaction brought home to us what it meant to other people.'

As so often happens in Gaelic football, the origins of Derry's historic triumph in 1993 can be traced to successes in earlier years. In particular, the county's All-Ireland minor successes in 1983 and 1989 were the springboard for all that would follow. From 1989 came names like Dermot Heaney and Gary Coleman, although it was another young star who really caught the eye. He did so not alone for his majestic football skills but also for his commanding frame of over 6 ft 4 in. It wouldn't be long before he would make his mark as one of the finest midfielders in Gaelic football history. His name was Anthony Tohill.

A player with the Swatragh club, Anthony Tohill arrived at an exciting time for Ulster football. After decades in the wilderness, the province was once again competing with the finest and showing a remarkable propensity for winning. Having lived for so long in the shadow of Kerry, Dublin, Meath and Cork, Ulster counties were back with a vengeance. In 1991 Down had captured the All-Ireland title. The following year, Donegal repeated the trick. Throughout that time, Derry were drawing from the minor panels of 1983 and 1989 and blending youth and experience into a potent football mix. To seasoned observers, it seemed just about right that Derry should follow Down and Donegal into the pantheon of worthy All-Ireland winners.

'The success of the other Ulster counties in the early 1990s really triggered us,' Anthony says. 'We saw what they could do. In 1991 we took Down to a replay. Down were very fortunate to get a replay against us with a rather dubiously awarded free kick. I was at the game when Down won the All-Ireland that year. In Ulster there's always been a sort of sense that when a team goes down to represent the province at All-Ireland level, the majority of people get behind them. But as a player there's a part of you that feels this could have been us. While I was in some way glad, I wasn't ecstatic that Down won. I was glad because I knew a few of the players and I was happy for them. But the overriding emotion for me was that it could have been us and that we were good enough to go and achieve what they had done.

'To be truthful about it, I don't think if it had been Derry that we'd have won an All-Ireland in '91. Certainly, having seen Down do it, when we came back in '92 we were very keen and we knew that we were good enough to win an All-Ireland. Unfortunately, all we ended up with was the league, but it was still a very important part of our development. Winning a National Football League, the first national title Derry had won for years, was a huge boost to us. It meant a lot more then than it means now. Also, having got to an Ulster final against Donegal we knew we were good enough but we fell a wee bit short that day.

'I didn't attend the All-Ireland final in '92 when Donegal won because I had a friend who needed a ticket more than I did and I was happy to oblige. But I was happy for Donegal. I recognised the work that they put in. They had been knocking on the door for a few years previous to that. Maybe Derry were still at the development stage but again the overriding emotion was that this could have been us and possibly should have been us. It galvanised your energy and it certainly made you more determined for the following year to make sure that you were going to do everything it took to win the All-Ireland.'

Anthony Tohill and his Derry team-mates had every reason to be optimistic about the 1993 championship. They were worthy National Football League winners in 1992, having defeated Tyrone in the final. They started the 1993 Ulster championship with a resounding victory over Down. That day, Anthony Tohill turned in one of his huge performances. He was again at the centre of Derry's Ulster semi-final win over Monaghan, setting up a provincial decider against the reigning All-Ireland champions, Donegal. The final took place on a wet, miserable day in Clones, with conditions that were widely described as unplayable. Out of the muck and slush Derry emerged as worthy winners, with Anthony Tohill again the powerhouse behind his team's victory. That was the day when he took the game by the scruff of the neck and almost single-handedly engineered Derry's great triumph.

'Certainly, weather-wise it was an appalling day but if you were a Derry supporter it was a marvellous day,' Anthony recalls. 'Maybe, in hindsight, the game shouldn't have been played in the conditions. But the powers-that-be took a decision to play the game and certainly at the final whistle we weren't complaining. It was a relief that we had won the Ulster title after being close in the two previous years. It was a massive achievement for us and I suppose it was another important stepping stone on the road to our All-Ireland success.

'It wasn't a day for spectacular football or fancy football. It was a day for grinding out a result. I think we were slightly down at half-time and we got a good lift from our management. At the start of the second half we knew that we had to up our game. I suppose sometime during that game it clicked with me that rather than kicking the ball up the pitch, possibly the best way was to start to carry it. We probably had the physical strength over the Donegal players and on that occasion we were able to carry the ball up the pitch and grind out scores. Through our greater strength or maybe our greater hunger and will to win, we drove up the pitch in numbers and took the game to them and got the couple of scores that mattered. On that day, it went for us.'

Throughout the Ulster championship campaign of 1993, Anthony Tohill got his first real chance to prove himself in the Derry midfield and it was an opportunity he was determined not to forego. The previous year he had played out on the wing, in the right half-forward position. His performances prompted the Derry management team, led by manager Éamonn Coleman, to switch him to centre-field, where he slotted in alongside Brian McGilligan. With McGilligan playing a more physical, holding role, Tohill ran with the ball, tearing defences apart and chalking up vital scores for his county. It was a role he would thrive in during the 1993 campaign.

Having passed their test in Ulster, Derry faced Dublin in the All-Ireland semi-final. With only one championship semi-final victory achieved in the history of Derry football, the prospects were far from promising. Clearly the underdogs, Derry emerged victorious after a heart-stopping game, scoring in the closing minutes to squeeze past Dublin by 0–15 to 0–14. 'It was a tough battle,' as Anthony puts it, 'but certainly it was no great surprise to us when we won it, such was the belief in the squad. There was a great burden of expectation upon the Dublin side but we went into the game with a belief that we were going to win. We never entertained getting beaten and I suppose that was to the great credit of our management that they instilled that belief in us. There was no way we were going to be stopped by any county.'

Cork were Derry's opponents in the All-Ireland final. The scene was set for a battle of the two red-and-white counties. Derry were going for their first-ever championship title. Cork were going for their seventh. Euphoria gripped the city and county of Derry. It was a football-mad county in a football-mad province and the scramble for tickets was unprecedented. Cork started well and burst into the lead. Then Cork's Tony Davis was sent off. Derry led at half-time. In the second half, Cork slipped into the lead. Next came a Derry revival and the realisation of a long-cherished dream. Scenes of jubilation greeted the final whistle as Derry won by 1–14 to 2–8. For the first time in history, the Sam Maguire Cup was brought home to Derry.

'We had a job to do and we weren't going down to Dublin to the All-Ireland final to make up the numbers,' Anthony recalls. 'We were going down to win and to do that you have to remain very focused. We hadn't been in an All-Ireland final since 1958, there was a great buzz around the county and it would have been easy for some players to get distracted by that. But our management kept our feet on the ground and there was determination amongst the players that we weren't going to allow the occasion to get to us. We were very mindful that we were there to carry out a job and that we needed to keep our focus.

'The bus picked us up in Maghera and there were quite a few people to see us off. The whole way down, there was a cavalcade of Derry cars going to the game. In towns that we went through, people were out wishing us well. You had to sort of look at it but not let it sink in and not let it affect you. Our focus was on the job in hand and we weren't going to let those festivities get in the way. We'll sit back in years to come and reflect on it, it was just a massive occasion for everyone in the county.

'We stayed out at the Airport Hotel. Leaving the hotel, one of the fellows had a tape of high-tempo dance music, which we played on the bus going to the games, and that sort of blanked everything out. You couldn't hear yourself think, never mind anything else. Going in to the ground in those days you had to walk in under the Hogan Stand and you were walking through supporters. At the minute, you can get in under the Cusack Stand with the buses and you don't really see supporters. Supporters were there wishing you all the best and all that was on your mind was getting into the dressing-room and getting togged out. Once we got out on to the pitch, all the nerves dissipated and it was a matter of getting on with the job.

'We couldn't have got off to a worse start. I don't know whether that was down to nerves or inexperience of Croke Park or just a wee bit of luck in terms of Cork getting the break and scoring a goal. To find yourself five points down after less than ten minutes in an All-Ireland final wasn't very encouraging. When things like that happen early in the game, you have plenty of time not to panic and to settle down. I think it was Johnny McGurk got our first point a few minutes later and it was a very important score. It was something that Johnny had been doing for us all year, popping up and getting crucial scores. That settled us and once we had the first point on the board, we knew the game was still very much to be played for.

'The Tony Davis sending-off was one of the turning points. I think the cameras would have shown that it possibly should have been someone else that should have got sent off for an earlier infringement. Maybe that was weighing on the mind of the referee when he saw the tackle that Tony made. You never like to see a player getting sent off in any game and especially in an All-Ireland final. To miss out on that through being sent off is very disappointing for the player involved but it also would have upset Cork. It gave us a spare man and it was Johnny McGurk who was given the role. He certainly had a big bearing on us winning the game.

'We got back into the game before half-time and in the second half the rain came down and things started to get a wee bit messy in terms of handling the ball. I remember distinctly Cork getting their second goal. The second goal really put them back in the driving seat and despite being a man down they were playing very committed football. At that stage we were beginning to wonder whether we were going to get there at the final whistle. But the resilience we had built up over that year and the previous years stood to us. With Henry Downey and Johnny McGurk driving us through from the half-back line, we just managed to get the few scores that counted towards the end.

'It was just pure relief when the whistle went. I think that was my overriding emotion. Cork had attacked and they had a "50", which I tried to convince the umpire was out for a wide. It was a "50" and it was chipped in. The ball broke loose and we picked it up and we were coming out with the ball. We were all defending like our lives depended on it. Then the final whistle went. I was elated, but I was elated because I was relieved that everything was over and we had done it. I know that for me the fear of losing was always a bigger thing than the actual prospect of winning. To know that you hadn't failed was a huge relief. At that particular moment that outweighed the actual joy that you had got through winning the All-Ireland.

'The scenes that unfolded, especially back in those days when supporters were allowed on to the pitch, were just marvellous for everyone associated with the team. I remember I met my dad underneath the Hogan Stand and I just wondered how he got from the safety of the Hogan Stand out into this madness that was going on out on the pitch. All I was saying to him was: "Dad, get out of here, get back up to the stands in case you get trampled on." It was just sheer madness. But they were good memories and it's something that I'll look back on in later life.'

Although it ranks as the pinnacle of his time in football, the winning of the All-Ireland final in 1993 didn't rate as the greatest performance of Anthony Tohill's career. Nor, indeed, was his performance in the All-Ireland semi-final against Dublin a match for his finest games in a Derry jersey. As it happened, he almost missed the semi-final through injury and his fitness in the final was curtailed through the slow process of recuperation. A perfectionist by nature, he always aspired to play better. In retrospect, however, Anthony Tohill should probably never have made the team against Dublin and was an outside chance to be fit for the final against Cork.

'On the Monday night before we played Dublin in the All-Ireland semi-final, we were training and I went up to catch a ball and landed on my ankle,' Anthony remembers. 'I was a severe doubt for the semi-final. I couldn't train that week. On the Friday before the game I was able to do a fast walk; that was about as good as I could do. I went out the night before the Dublin game with our team doctor to do a fitness test. We jogged around the field a little bit and my ankle was hurting like hell. "How is it?" he asked me. "It's all right," I said. There was no way I was going to miss the game. I felt that once I got out there, in the heat of the moment I'd soon forget about my injury.

'Playing the Dublin game after getting injured meant that for two weeks after the game I couldn't train. I missed out on a wee bit of fitness work and when it came to the All-Ireland final there were certain runs that I would like to have made that I didn't feel I had the legs for. But when you win, the last thing you worry about is how you play yourself. What matters is the team, and that day the team won. That's all that matters.'

For his achievements in football, Anthony Tohill won four All-Star awards. He won another Ulster championship medal in 1998 to add to the first he won in '93. He also shared in Derry's remarkable run of league successes, winning 4 National Football League medals. In addition, as an 18 year old in 1990 he played for a time in Australia, having moved there on a scholarship to play Australian Rules football. Fortunately, he was back in time for Derry's great championship run that eventually secured the county's historic All-Ireland title in 1993. It was a showcase championship campaign that brought to attention one of the finest midfielders in Gaelic football history, a player who demonstrated his skills at the height of Ulster's finest years.

'It was a glorious period for Ulster football,' Anthony concludes. 'There was Down in 1991 and '94, ourselves in '93 and Donegal in '92. Then there was Tyrone coming within a kick of a ball of winning it in '95. The fact that it spanned across four different counties makes it that wee bit special. It wasn't one county dominating; you had four counties that were capable of winning an All-Ireland and three of them did. Since then, Armagh and Tyrone have shown us that teams from Ulster can compete and be as good if not better than any other sides throughout Ireland.

'The early 1990s were for me the golden years for Ulster football. That Derry squad that won the All-Ireland was no doubt capable of winning another one but unfortunately it didn't happen. In fairness to Derry, since '93 we tried to replicate that success but there were a number of things that happened. Looking back at it now, I think it was a marvellous achievement but we would dearly like to have won another one. I suppose it's a double-edged emotion; you're grateful that you did it but at the same time you're a bit disappointed that you didn't do it again.'